Writing in Education

Teaching Writing

Series Editor

Patricia Leavy (*USA*)

VOLUME 8

The titles published in this series are listed at *brill.com/writ*

Writing in Education

The Art of Writing for Educators

By

Elizabeth Chase, Nancy P. Morabito and
Sandra Schamroth Abrams

Foreword by Peter Smagorinsky

BRILL

SENSE

LEIDEN | BOSTON

All chapters in this book have undergone peer review.

Library of Congress Cataloging-in-Publication Data

Names: Chase, Elizabeth (Liz), author. | Morabito, Nancy Pierce, author. | Abrams, Sandra Schamroth, author.
Title: Writing in education : the art of writing for educators / by Elizabeth Chase, Nancy P. Morabito and Sandra Schamroth Abrams.
Description: Leiden ; Boston : Brill Sense, 2020. | Series: Teaching writing, 2542-9698 ; volume 8 | Includes bibliographical references and index.
Identifiers: LCCN 2020028816 (print) | LCCN 2020028817 (ebook) | ISBN 9789004437241 (Paperback : acid-free paper) | ISBN 9789004437258 (Hardback : acid-free paper) | ISBN 9789004437265 (eBook)
Subjects: LCSH: Education--Authorship. | Academic writing. | Teachers as authors. | Educational publishing.
Classification: LCC LB1033.5 .C445 2020 (print) | LCC LB1033.5 (ebook) | DDC 808.02--dc23
LC record available at https://lccn.loc.gov/2020028816
LC ebook record available at https://lccn.loc.gov/2020028817

ISSN 2542-9698
ISBN 978-90-04-43724-1 (paperback)
ISBN 978-90-04-43725-8 (hardback)
ISBN 978-90-04-43726-5 (e-book)

This book is printed on acid-free paper and produced in a sustainable manner.

ADVANCE PRAISE FOR
WRITING IN EDUCATION: THE ART OF WRITING FOR EDUCATORS

"The professional writing you do as an educator matters. *Writing in Education: The Art of Writing for Educators,* a unique text for our field, supports PK-12 educators to write with intention. The ideas, examples, and thoughtful questions posed throughout the text will guide teachers and teacher candidates to refine their writing craft for a wide variety of stakeholders and purposes. Drs. Chase, Morabito, and Abrams share their expertise to help educators write with knowledge, confidence, and power."
– Denise N. Morgan, Ph.D., Professor, Literacy Education, Kent State University

"A must-read for everyone interested in the teaching of writing, Chase, Morabito, and Abrams have written a text that speaks to teachers, teacher candidates, and teacher educators. This book invites an engagement in provocative strategies and tools that help teachers think through and practice multiple forms of writing—from deep reflection to multimodal exploration, to certification-based reporting, and communicating with various stakeholders. It is a meaningful and practical guide that brings a fresh perspective to the art of and craft of teaching writing in online and in-person classrooms."
– Yolanda Sealey-Ruiz, Ph.D., Associate Professor, English Education, Teachers College, Columbia University, author of *Love from the Vortex & Other Poems*

"In *Writing in Education: The Art of Writing for Educators,* Chase, Morabito, and Abrams make the powerful—and too often neglected—argument that being a teacher requires being a writer. This book points the way for how teachers can do professional writing that benefits themselves and, more importantly, their students."
– Michael W. Smith, Ph.D., Professor, Department of Teaching and Learning, Temple University, co-author of *Developing Writers of Argument: Tools & Rules That Sharpen Students' Reasoning*

To my students, who have come into my life and shown me better ways.
To my family, whose love and support transcend boundaries.
– Liz

To my students, whose spirit and creativity continuously shape my own teaching and learning.
To my family, for their boundless support and love.
– Nancy

To my students, for their inspiring craft.
To my family, for their their endearing warmth and enduring love.
– Sandra

CONTENTS

PETER SMAGORINSKY

FOREWORD

When I began my doctoral studies in 1983, I was teaching in the English Department at Barrington (IL) High School in the suburbs of Chicago. We had recently been treated to a visit from Janet Emig—a former professor of my department chair's when they had both been at the University of Chicago in the 1960s—and her supporting cast from Rutgers. They provided a workshop they'd developed through the New Jersey Writing Project in which we were encouraged to view ourselves as writers, mostly of highly personal, vividly voiced narratives. We were in turn encouraged to teach our students to take on the identities of committed, engaging writers who explored their own experiences through reflection and narrative. I'd also been influenced by an educational history I'd just read that had included a jaunty, conversational, appealing voice. I was ready to begin my doctoral studies with George Hillocks at the University of Chicago, eager to write in ways that were expressive, insightful, well-wrought, and thought-provoking.

My first semester of doctoral studies included a class taught by Charles Bidwell, a distinguished sociologist of education with a seeming life-long association with the university, one that included all of his academic degrees and a long term on the faculty, spanning seven decades at the time of his death. At semester's end I submitted my paper, confident that by dressing my ideas in highly stylized prose, I would make a favorable impression on Professor Bidwell. That assurance took a hard hit when he returned my paper. His only response was, "You don't write like a scholar."

Before his appraisal of my lack of scholarly chops, I'd developed the identity of a writer who brought smiles to the faces of my appreciative English department colleagues through my clever and witty narratives. After this assessment from a titan of sociology whose opprobrious countenance suggested that I would never make it in this business, I felt like a rank amateur. I declared a mission to learn how to write like a social science scholar of the sort envisioned by my professors in Judd Hall. I finally caught on, but it was a long and bumpy journey that involved shifts in both my prose and my sense of self as an educator and author.

Which brings me to this unique new book about teachers and writing. *Writing in Education: The Art of Writing for Educators* provides something that to my knowledge has yet to grace the profession: a book that helps teachers know what sort of professional writing to anticipate, and how to produce it. Not necessarily the lively, expressive writing I'd learned to produce through my Writing Project experiences, or the less animated prose I then learned to generate for my scholarship. Rather, this book is designed to help teachers write the sorts of texts that their careers will demand, usually learned on their own, often with naïve assumptions and phrasings that produce unintended consequences.

As a teacher from 1976–1990, I wrote many things, mostly with a pen on the back of discarded paper. I used an electric typewriter for formal letters and lessons headed for the mimeograph machine. I finally got my first computer in the late 1980s as a gift from my parents so I could write my dissertation.

But most of my teacherly writing was done by hand. I wrote lengthy comments on students' writing. I participated in my annual reviews, writing to verify the observer's impressions of my teaching. I wrote gobs of lessons and activities that I shared with my students and colleagues, and in some cases the profession through presentations and publications. I "wrote up" the occasional uncooperative student, and wrote letters to newspapers on educational issues in the news. I wrote letters to people to stay in touch, short stories and satires that occasionally got published, proposals to conferences and subsequently papers that served as both conference presentations and journal articles, and other texts great and small. And then while teaching and attending graduate school, I also learned how to write like a scholar.

Each genre I wrote in required different rhetorical understandings. I needed to know what sort of text I was producing, what expectations accompanied such texts, and which readers' sensibilities I needed to address. I learned much of what I knew about differentiating my writing according to task, genre, and readership on my own, or through feedback from either critical friends or the recipients of my texts. There was nothing like the university course that inspired *Writing in Education: The Art of Writing for Educators*, one that helps teachers learn the various sorts of writing that they might need to do as part of their work. They probably learn (or so I hope!) to write lessons, units, and activities in their teacher education programs. They might be shepherded through the writing required on a performance assessment required for certification; I've provided some guidelines on this task myself (Smagorinsky, 2018), although as a byproduct of learning how to design instruction.

What teachers rarely get is what this book provides: Explicit attention to the rhetorical demands of different tasks, genres, and readers for the writing that teachers do as part of their jobs. My studies with George Hillocks (e.g., Hillocks, 1995) had impressed on me the task-related needs of writing in different genres. Writing a letter to educational stakeholders, writing in relation to tasks on a performance assessment, writing in response to students' writing: All are writing, but of very different sorts. Each calls for different language, different syntax, different degrees of formality, different sources of evidence, and much more (Bazerman & Paradis, 1989). I've been told periodically that "writing is writing is writing." But it ain't.

This book assumes that it helps for teachers to know, learn how to produce, and practice the types of writing that will be expected of them in their work, and perhaps in the extension of their work into other areas of life. The authors position writing as an art through which meaning-making may become available. Meaningfulness may not be available in all of the writing that teachers do; some is bureaucratic and empty of personal meaning. But it is available when the writer is seeking to communicate, express, persuade, narrate, and so on. This value on meaningfulness benefits from appropriate knowledge and use of conventions, either to follow or violate, with attention to the rhetorical situation in which the writing will be read. Writing is thus, as Miller (1984) argued, a tool used in service of social action within the contours of a genre, and so must involve more than knowledge of a formalist set of features.

This volume provides beginning teachers (or veterans who find it enticing) with strategies for producing many of the sorts of texts that teachers tend to write. Whether for university-based, certification-oriented performance assessments or for on-the-job evaluations such as NBPTS certification, the authors provide guidance in writing teacher reflections in relation to video documentation or other evidence of effective teaching. Readers also get guidance in reflective writing on their teaching outside the bounds of formal assessment. They learn how to write to stakeholders, including families, administrators, school boards, and other invested parties. They get suggestions for how to write aspects of instructional planning, from articulating objectives, to writing rationales for units of study, to response to student writing, and more. They also learn to produce texts that involve more than words, such as digital media narratives about teaching, and reflections on such productions.

The volume can't prepare prospective and practicing teachers for everything, but then, no text could anticipate every need. What the authors provide is attention to a solid set of writing tasks common to many teachers, and guidelines for how to produce texts that are *in tune* with the situation and their readers, as Nystrand (1986) once phrased the manner in which good writing enables communication with readers rather than embodying a static, autonomous set of qualities that apply to all writing. As my opening vignette indicates, writers' relationships with their readers and the community of practice they inhabit determines whether writing is good or not. That's a sensibility that benefits from the sort of teaching that the authors provide in this unique volume, one that deserves a place in teacher education programs where writing matters. It also should benefit practicing teachers whose work entails writing in different genres and tasks, and whose understanding of how to read their readers' sensibilities often determines the extent to which an act of communication has succeeded. It's a great idea, well-executed, and no doubt bound to help a lot of teachers with this fundamental, yet long-overlooked, dimension of a teaching life.

REFERENCES

Bazerman, C., & Paradis, J. (Eds.). (1989). *Textual dynamics of the professions: Historical and contemporary studies of writing in professional communities*. University of Wisconsin Press.

Hillocks, G. (1995). *Teaching writing as reflective practice*. Teachers College Press.

Miller, C. R. (1984). Genre as social action. *Quarterly Journal of Speech, 70*, 151–167.

Nystrand, M. (1986). *The structure of written communication: Studies in reciprocity between writers and readers*. Brill.

Smagorinsky, P. (2018). *Teaching English by design: How to create and carry out instructional units* (2nd ed.). Heinemann.

Peter Smagorinsky
Department of Language and Literacy Education
The University of Georgia

ACKNOWLEDGMENTS

This book is part of the *Teaching Writing* series, and we thank the series editor, Dr. Patricia Leavy, for offering us the opportunity to share our insights with the field. Likewise, we appreciate Shalen Lowell's work as the assistant to Dr. Patricia Leavy. We also acknowledge the Brill | Sense staff who make publication possible; thank you, John Bennett and Jolanda Karada and the rest of the Brill | Sense publication team. Furthermore, we extend gratitude to Peter Smagorinsky, whose expertise and perspectives in the Foreword offer an important dimension to the text and provide additional context for writing in education.

This endeavor came to fruition with the support of our St. John's University colleagues and our individual families. In particular, we appreciate the intellectual freedom, time, and space to develop and refine the course—*The Art of Writing for Educators*—that has served as the inspiration for this book. We especially thank our colleague, Dr. Judith Mangione, who supported the inception of this course many years ago and shared our vision for crafting an experience for our students to explore writing in education. We also thank our Dean, Dr. David Bell, for his encouragement and support. Finally, writing is a humbling process that involves countless hours of work, and we acknowledge and appreciate the myriad ways our partners and children have endured the process with us. Balancing the rearing of children and the rearing of a book is no easy feat, and the patience and support we have received from our immediate and extended families has made it possible for us to complete this manuscript *and* enjoy time with loved ones. Thank you!

We are grateful for our many students, past and present, whose writings, reflections, and commentaries have helped to shape the initial conception and content of this book. We have grown alongside our students, refining and developing our practice over many semesters. We truly appreciate the feedback and insights that our students have shared over the years, and we are honored to showcase examples inspired by their work.

FIGURES

INTRODUCTION

Writing in school typically conjures images of students sitting at desks, either with pen in hand or fingers on a keyboard, composing *something* in response to a prompt. Typing "writing and school" into a Google Images search box yields an endless series of this exact picture: students at desks, quietly folded over pen and paper. This image suggests that writing is experienced alone, that it is confined to prompts and responses, and that its boundaries are the extent of the page. Although this is one interpretation of writing, it is not ours. Rather, we prefer to think of writing as an artform unto itself. We see writing as a conduit to growth, a meaningful engagement with self and with multimodal texts, and, as evidenced by this book, we see it as an important practice for professional educators.

Writing in Education: The Art of Writing for Educators focuses on educators' professional journeys and discoveries about teaching, learning, writing, and self. To that end, this book offers insightful discussions about teaching practices, engaging examinations of digital representations of meaning, and thoughtful explorations of reflective writing. At the same time, this book maintains a close eye on practical matters facing teachers and teacher candidates, be it writing beyond the content areas or conducting classroom observations and maintaining field notes. Although our discussions and descriptions focus on practices and standards in U.S. classrooms, the topics and concepts are universal and can be adapted and applied to international settings and standards. In this Introduction, we take you on a narrative journey as we explain the impetus for and approach to crafting this book and the important information you can find within it.

PART ONE: WHAT WE NOTICED

As life-long educators, we bring an extensive history of teaching experience to this book. Among the three of us, we have a combined total of more than 50 years teaching in PK-12 and higher education classrooms. We have been fourth grade classroom teachers, high school science and English teachers, middle school math and English teachers, and college professors spanning multiple content areas. All of these experiences have enabled us to observe and engage with students as writers in a variety of contexts. We have learned so much about writing over the course of our years as educators and as educational researchers; perhaps the greatest lesson is that learning to write effectively is an on-going process that never really ends.

Much of this book is based on the collective work we have engaged in as professors of a course that is this book's namesake, *The Art of Writing for Educators*. In Fall 2013, Nancy and Sandra incepted and co-taught the first of many sections of *The Art of Writing for Educators*. Since that time, Liz and Nancy have co-taught the course, and Liz and Sandra have taught it individually. What we have found through the process of developing and teaching the course informs this book and inspires us to bring the ideas to a wider audience through this text.

The initial impetus for developing the writing course for educators was our observation that our students were struggling with the writing section of a (then) newly implemented teaching assessment, the Education Teacher Performance Assessment, which is more commonly known as the edTPA. We noticed that many of our education students needed to develop their writing skills, and we needed a dedicated class to help them hone these skills in a practical way. We envisioned a course vastly different from the options that already existed: traditional university expository writing courses, creative writing courses in an English department, and writing methods courses (e.g., how to teach writing) within an Education department. Instead, our course's focus was on effective practices in the field of education, examinations and discussions of teaching and learning, and connections between education theory and classroom practice. Ultimately, we wanted to support our students' (a) understanding of writing, (b) their ability to write professionally in the field of education, and (c) their ability to consider the implications of such knowledge and skills for their own future teaching. To that end, we crafted a course that invited our teacher candidates to think about and develop the kinds of writing experiences they would professionally engage in *and* that they likely would extend to their future students.

This course offered our students unique opportunities to refine skills while writing about experiences in and beyond the classroom and to make connections between theory and the practice. This helped students (re)consider their instructional beliefs and approaches while also developing a language with which to discuss what actually occurred in a classroom, why it was relevant, and how it could be developed even further in the future. We find that we are not alone in our determination that real-world connections are crucially important in writing instruction. Researchers Meghan Barnes and Peter Smagorinsky (2016) examined three different English Language Arts teacher education programs and found that not one of them had courses that specifically included "real-world relevance" in their coursework (p. 12). This is troubling, and it is something that, coincidentally, we wanted to address in our coursework.

Curriculum Matters: Teacher Education

Teacher education programs are designed to prepare teacher candidates for their forthcoming roles as classroom educators. Although the content of teacher education programs in the United States varies, Barnes and Smagorinsky (2016) found common features among three different US university teacher education programs, and not one of the topics included professional writing for educators.

Specifically, their research found that elementary education teacher candidates with a concentration in English (or Language Arts):

> emerged from coursework well-versed in *ELA teaching principles*, such as instructional planning, teaching writing, assessing student work, and other basic responsibilities of the job. They also, either through generalizations from these principles in courses or from mentorship elsewhere, learned what we considered to be *general teaching principles,* e.g., classroom management, appropriate instruction in light of human development and other factors, and a wide range of other principles shared by teachers across the curriculum. In addition to talking about what they did learn, the teacher candidates also noted holes in their preparation, which we classified as *information not learned in practicum and information not learned in coursework,* categories that included how to apply technology, how to move theory into practice, and other matters not covered extensively in coursework or fieldwork. Finally, the teacher candidates learned about what we classified as the *educational landscape of teaching,* a non-pedagogical category that included attention to the context of teaching, traits of communities, and other non-pedagogical aspects of the profession that influence instructional decisions. (Barnes & Smagorinsky, 2016, p. 5)

Although we believe teacher education programs attend to students' needs, we also recognize that these needs evolve. We offer this text with hope that teachers and teacher candidates will have the opportunity to learn about and refine their own professional writing in education.

Although we are all university professors, we still see ourselves as students of writing. We might be tasked with teaching college students how to develop their writing skills so that they can communicate effectively and concisely, but we are learners first and foremost. Each new course is an opportunity to explore writing processes with our students, and each new assignment is an opportunity for us to develop our own feedback to more effectively help writers grow and flourish. We write this book in response to an identified need in the field; frankly, there are few books that address what we refer to as, *The Art of Writing for Educators.*

Without question, there are heaps of books on how to teach writing in PK-12 classrooms, but there are few resources that help teachers and teacher candidates develop their own professional writing skills. Each semester, as we prepared to teach our writing course, we wanted and needed a text that would support the kind of teaching we would engage in for that course. Primarily, we wanted a text that would help teacher candidates develop stronger writing skills for their work in the field of education. With a dearth of options to which we could turn, we saw that there was a need for this particular kind of text in the field, so we decided to write our own.

PART TWO: WHAT WE DID

Although we initially approached this book with teacher candidates in mind, we intend for it to serve as a useful resource for anyone pursuing a career in education. The topics and examples are aligned to work that we all do as educators, such as rationalizing pedagogy, writing within and beyond content areas, and engaging in reflective writing. We believe that the content offered in this book can be tailored to serve a wide variety of people in the field of education, from teacher candidates, to practicing teachers, to administrators. Writing is an extremely important part of the work of educators. And, more importantly, our writing behaviors and products serve as powerful examples for the students we teach. We agree with Morgan and Pytash (2014), among others, that one way to suggest a culture of writing in your classroom is to model the behaviors and actions of a writer yourself.

This text offers unique sightlines into the kinds of writing that educators are asked to perform. Specifically, this book explores everything from reflective writing in education to writing for performance-based assessments. As such, this book offers something for a variety of audiences at different stages in their educational and professional trajectories. For current students of education, we envision this book serving as a support for honing writing skills overall, increasing awareness of the writing demands of the teaching profession, and preparing teachers to be effective communicators. This book also would be particularly useful to classroom educators who want to think about these same topics more deeply, or who might need some support in a specific task, whether it be drafting a letter to a principal, preparing a write-up for a national board certification assessment, or engaging in reflective examinations of classroom practice. Thus, it is important to develop ourselves as writers within the field of education.

Although we offer exemplars and suggestions for writing and writing instruction, we do so understanding that no text is neutral. Drawing upon work by Brian Street (1999), as well as constructivist notions that we all build upon our experiences, we recognize that readers approach and interpret any text—from a novel (e.g., alphabetic text, positioning of words on a page, presence of images) to the theatre (e.g., body language and positioning, gesture, voice inflection, costume) to a football field (e.g., player positioning, referee signals, oral communication, body language, noted boundaries and field markers)—through the lens of their experience. There are socioculturally situated "funds of knowledge" or "historically accumulated and culturally developed bodies of knowledge and skills" (Moll et al., 1992, p. 133) that contribute to one's understanding of self and of texts. Someone who has seen and held a conch shell, for example, automatically would know its texture, its appearance, and perhaps even its potential as a trumpeting instrument, thus providing a layer of understanding for its significance in Caribbean musical expression (Murdoch, 2009) and its presence in William Golding's *Lord of the Flies*. Furthermore, someone familiar with a conch likely would know that it is pronounced "konk"[1] and not "con-ch" and that the shell was once the home to a sea creature.

Texts also are not neutral because they are context-specific, even if they have universal themes. One of the reasons English teachers explore the historical setting of a book and the author's background is to provide a context for the text at hand. George Orwell's novel, *1984*, which addresses extreme government surveillance, oppression, and control, might have been published after the Second World War, but it has contemporary implications and applications. *How* a reader interprets those connections depends on the reader's own experiences, as well as the reader's knowledge of current and historical political situations. In 1946, Orwell (or, rather, Eric Blair—George Orwell was a pen name) published the essay, *Why I Write*, in which he traced his development as a writer first to his boyhood and his penchant for language and writing and then to his various experiences with and awareness of poverty and political ills. Orwell specifically explained to readers the purpose of the essay: "I give all this background information because I do not think one can assess a writer's motives without knowing something of his early development" (2005, p. 4). We encourage all readers—even if they are outside the field of education—to think about the roots of their personal interpretation of a text *and* how their writing draws from their funds of knowledge and deeply-rooted contextualized meanings.

We also encourage readers to be mindful of their previous *and* current experiences when reading texts that specifically express social, cultural, and even political messages. For example, Langston Hughes's *Let America Be America Again*, published in 1936 in *Esquire Magazine*, juxtaposes the promise of what America could be with the inequities and injustices that regrettably still continue to plague American society 84 years later. Your own interpretations and experiences might inform how you read and understand Hughes's poem. Couple these interpretations with others' perspectives of the poem, and the collective understandings can create a rich knowledge that honors the context and content *and* also generates important sensitivities and awareness.

We call specific attention to the lack of neutrality to underscore the highly nuanced nature of writing, interpretation, and, of course, teaching. There is no "one size fits all" model, nor should there be. Readers will come to this text and take from it what they will. However, as we know from Louise Rosenblatt (1994), the reader interacts with a text and a text interacts with the reader. Therefore, when considering how writers and readers construct meaning, we need to acknowledge how genres reveal sociocultural behavior, norms, and expectations and how "writing is always an event in time... always embodying both personal and social, or individual and environmental, factors" (Rosenblatt, 1994, p. 1072). Writing for a culturally and linguistically diverse population of readers (as you might do as a teacher when writing to/ for administrators, families, and students) means being aware of *what* you write, *how* you write it, and the myriad ways your readers might interpret what you write. This is not to frighten you; rather, it is a reminder that no language is neutral because meaning is contextual and socioculturally situated. In other words, how you interpret a text can be vastly different from how others do, and such variation creates opportunity—it is what we do with that variation in meaning that matters. How teachers and teacher candidates create sensitivity and responsiveness to others' words, experiences, and interpretations is key, and reflection can support a reader's understanding of self in relation to the text.

Likewise, there is power and privilege in writing—it is important to consider not only who says what to whom, but also who is listening. It is also important to consider the historical implications of literacy and access to reading and writing instruction. For instance, during the era of slavery, educating African Americans was discouraged at best, and in many Southern states, it was illegal (Anderson, 1988). This period of enforced illiteracy was a way to use the written word as a gatekeeper for enslaved African Americans. And yet, enslaved African Americans employed other types of literacies, such as oral storytelling, to develop rich and nuanced ways of communicating among one another as well as from generation to generation. In this way, enslaved African Americans drew on funds of knowledge (Moll et al., 1992) to renegotiate the boundaries around their enforced illiteracy. We use this example to illustrate the complicated ways that power and privilege are intertwined with writing and to draw attention to the nuances of power and privilege to be explored with students.

This book is not about a tokenistic understanding that writing can produce and reproduce power. Rather, this book helps teachers and teacher candidates think expansively and deeply about opportunities to improve both their writing and teaching, acknowledging that readers will build upon their own funds of knowledge as they encounter the ideas and activities featured in this book.

Our goal in writing this book is to provide teachers and teacher candidates with tools and resources to refine their overall writing skills *and* to prepare (or strengthen) their writing for the unique context of professional, educational settings. Although we provide suggestions throughout this book about the mechanics of writing in such settings, our primary focus is not a "how to" of writing. Instead, we dedicate most of our efforts to (a) describing important forms of writing that teachers typically engage in, and (b) exploring how immersion in such writing can shape one's understanding of teaching and learning.

This being said, you will notice that one form of writing is *not* addressed in this book: the writing of lesson plans. Please be assured that this is not an oversight. We realize that the composition of lesson plans is often a focus of numerous other teacher education courses (e.g., teaching methods courses) and, as such, it already receives a lot of attention elsewhere. In fact, we do not address lesson planning in our *Art of Writing for Educators* course for this exact reason. Furthermore, there is such a vast range of approaches to structuring and writing lesson plans (frequently dictated by schools of education for the purposes of coursework, or by a district or school in which a teacher works), that it would be an insurmountable task to address the needs and/or requirements of all existing approaches to lesson planning. Instead, we envision the strategies and approaches for thinking about writing in educational settings that we *do* address—such as reflective writing, the composition of a digital story, or the construction of a portfolio—as being fully applicable for also thinking more deeply about the writing that goes into lesson planning and curriculum development.

PART THREE: THE WORK THAT RESULTED

The contents of this book are based largely upon the course framework that we have used while teaching *The Art of Writing for Educators*. Like our course, the text is divided into three main sections, with each of the chapters addressing a different aspect of writing. Each chapter includes a Featured Assignment, a vetted activity that we have updated and refined over the years and that integrates and exemplifies the core concepts addressed in the chapter. The Featured Assignment will help readers to home in on the specified form of writing and to practice the strategies and skills addressed in each chapter. For example, one of the Featured Assignments is a Portfolio Assignment, which offers a concrete and organized approach to identify, analyze, and synthesize growth, challenges, and opportunities for improvement in one's writing. Acknowledging development is extremely important, as is remaining vigilant of writing errors (e.g., tense shifts, punctuation, telling not showing) that might surface in current and future work. If this text is being used for a teacher education or professional development course, we suggest that all of the Featured Assignments be used to support the development of teachers' and teacher candidates' understandings of writing.

Additionally, given that teaching, learning, and writing are multifaceted topics, we include *Curriculum Matters* spotlight boxes across the chapters. The information within the spotlight boxes offers supplementary *and* complementary points that inform, but do not interfere with, the primary topic of discussion. After all, curriculum does, indeed, *matter*, and there are certain *matters* for consideration that we have chosen to focus on in this book. Thus, readers can use the spotlight information to further their understanding of a topic—it is exciting to have an entrée to another perspective or a research study—and to remain continuously aware of the interconnectedness and complexity of teaching, learning, and writing.

We have found that it is helpful to begin our course by encouraging our teacher candidates to consider professional, written communication in educational settings. Therefore, Chapter 2, titled *Writing about Teaching and Learning*, highlights suggested practices for writing about teaching. Here we discuss using multiple sources of evidence to support one's claims, specifically addressing how a teacher might utilize this writing strategy to communicate with administrators and families to justify the use of a particular educational method or approach. We also consider how peer review can support teachers who want to improve their own writing. Additionally, we explore how writing about teaching can take many forms (e.g., teaching statements/philosophies, informal reflective notes, blogs), and we address formal examinations of teaching in the chapter's Featured Assignment: *Commenting on Teaching and Learning*. This assignment asks readers to watch a video clip of a teacher leading a lesson in a classroom, take notes about what is seen in the lesson, and then assume the role of the teacher in the video to compose written responses to the prompts provided. In so doing, readers have the opportunity to reflect upon and write about "their own" teaching in response to focused, guiding prompts.

In Chapter 3, *Expansive Writing beyond Content and Page*, we support readers in thinking about the different forms that writing can take both within and beyond the classroom. This is intended to encourage readers to develop (and strengthen existing) understandings of writing and literacy in relation to both their own writing and the writing in which their current or future students might engage. To do so, we address writing within and across content areas, as well as multiliteracies and cross-literate practices, to explore writing beyond alphabetic text. This chapter's Featured Assignment builds upon both the contents of the chapter *and* the highlighted practices addressed in Chapter 2 by asking the reader to compose a digital story examining writing in a variety of contexts. The *Digital Storytelling* assignment requires readers to work collaboratively to explore aspects of writing within and/or beyond classroom settings, then convey their understandings of writing and learning in these spaces through the development of a short video. The concluding aspect of this assignment asks readers to reflect upon the process of creating a digital story, as well as the potential utility of such a task for their current or future students.

Chapter 4 serves to tie all aspects of writing together and build upon them further through an extensive discussion of the role of teacher reflection and reflective writing. Titled *Reflecting on Reflective Practices*, this chapter begins by emphasizing the importance of teacher reflection and introduces the idea of reflection-in-writing and reflection-on-writing to underscore the role that writing can (and should) play in reflective teaching. We then explore these concepts further through a focused description of the role of field notes for reflection, with multiple suggestions for how to generate field notes (e.g., what should be included, logistical considerations) and how to use them productively (e.g., for class discussion, for reflecting on future practice). The Featured Assignment for this chapter, *The Portfolio*, draws upon these themes and the main themes of previous chapters by asking readers to "document how you have arrived at your current understandings" (p. 85) about writing through multiple iterations of reflection. Readers will curate a selection of writing based upon the assignments presented in this text (and possibly elsewhere) to communicate their ideas about writing. They will then reflect upon their shifting understandings of writing through analysis of their portfolio's contents, as well as through consideration of the implications and applications of these understandings for their own current or future teaching.

Addressing Language Use in This Text

In this book, you will notice the use of certain language to refer to different stakeholders in an educational environment. In this Introduction, we call attention to our discursive choices throughout the book to explain, instruct, and demonstrate how to respond to changing discursive practices within the educational landscape. First, we follow the conventions of the most recent version of American Psychological Association Publication Manual (i.e., APA 7) in using the pronoun "they/them" rather than "she/her" and "he/him." In cases where we are referencing the work of individuals whose gender identities were made known to us, we use the gender identities the individuals used to describe themselves.

Second, we rely on the terms *families, guardians,* and *caregivers* to reference the key stakeholders for students in PK-12 classrooms. In many instances, those stakeholders will be parents; however, this is not always the case. We suggest adopting language that does not rely on an assumption about the nature of the relationship between students and their caregivers. Terms such as *families, guardians,* or *caregivers* acknowledge the various compositions of families without assuming particular relationships. Further, terms such as these allow for a protective boundary around students who might have experienced the trauma of losing a parent or being separated from a parent.

Addressing Teaching Performance Assessments

This text will serve as a useful resource for teachers and teacher candidates who are preparing for certification exams. While these certification exams can vary by state, most states use the edTPA. This performance based assessment was created by the Stanford Center for Assessment, Learning and Equity and has been adopted by numerous states as a requirement for initial certification and licensure (see http://edtpa.aacte.org/?s=participation+map). Although many teacher candidates will prepare for the edTPA at some point in their teacher education program, not all candidates will have to complete this particular performance assessment. Thus, this text is not a preparation guide for the edTPA, nor is it a preparation guide for any particular type of certification assessment. It is, however, a valuable and useful tool for any educator who is considering (or undertaking) the demands of a performance-based assessment of teaching skills. A variety of exams, from the edTPA to the National Board for Professional Teaching Standards (NBPTS), require significant amounts of writing, and, in particular, reflective writing that demonstrates a teacher's ability to comment on and analyze teaching practices, evaluate student learning, and highlight areas for growth. This book supports teachers and teacher candidates who are working on developing their skills for clear, concise, and reflective writing. As such, this text can be used as one of many tools to support teachers and teacher candidates in their professional journeys.

CONCLUDING THOUGHTS

We hope that, taken together, the work in this book will increase your comfort and confidence as a writer in professional educational settings, expand your notions of what writing is and its role in a variety of contexts, and support you in becoming a (more) reflective practitioner. Even veteran teachers can benefit from taking time to think more deeply about their teaching, strengths, and areas for growth with respect to writing in professional contexts. Whether pursuing national board certification, serving as a mentor for a student teacher and wanting to model good writing practices, or simply trying to think of more effective means for communicating with families, there always is room for progress.

Furthermore, we aim to support current and future teachers of *all* grade levels and content areas. If you are a middle or high school math, social studies, art, music, or science teacher, you might be wondering how this book is relevant to you given that your courses do not traditionally have the focus upon writing that would be found in English classes at these grade bands. Truth be told, no matter what subject area you are responsible for teaching, you will undoubtedly engage in writing in some professional capacity. Overall, this book does not focus on strategies for *teaching* writing, but instead focuses on strategies for engaging *teachers and teacher candidates in improving their writing practices*.

NOTE

1 Please note the phonetic spelling is "Käŋk" per the dictionary by Merriam Webster.

WRITING ABOUT TEACHING AND LEARNING

GUIDING QUESTIONS

This chapter explores how to communicate your pedagogical strengths and philosophies through writing. As you read, please consider the following guiding questions, which are designed to support your journey through writing in education:

1. If you are a teacher, what are some teaching strategies that make you most proud? If you are a teacher candidate, what are some of the teaching strategies you already feel excited about trying in your future classroom?
2. Most teachers and teacher candidates will need to engage in the process of documenting and rationalizing their pedagogical strategies for the purposes of certification. What is the process in your state? For readers who already are certified at the state level, are you interested in pursuing National Board Certification? Knowing the answers to these questions can help you understand your professional requirements and provide further context for the ideas presented herein. Additionally, knowing your own certification requirements will help you determine what artifacts and writing samples you will need to collect and record.

INTRODUCTION

According to the 2017 National Assessment of Educational Progress (NAEP) Report Card, nationwide, only 28% of students in 4th grade, 8th grade and 12th grade scored "at or above proficient" in writing. These recent NAEP scores paint a portrait of a nation with only one-quarter of its students prepared to leave high school as proficient writers. Simultaneously, recent research has found that employers prioritize problem-solving skills, collaboration skills, and written communication skills as their top three attributes when hiring (Gray & Koncz, 2017). These two statistics suggest that supply does not meet demand. In other words, the data show that many high school seniors are graduating without the essential writing skills that are crucial for professional employment and success.

© ELIZABETH CHASE, NANCY P. MORABITO AND
SANDRA SCHAMROTH ABRAMS, 2020 | DOI: 10.1163/9789004437265_002

As professors, we see these realities play out in our higher education classrooms. Every semester, we encounter students who are quite masterful writers, while others struggle with the basics. Some students come prepared to compose text, provide feedback, and demonstrate their ideas in a variety of formats, while other students are most comfortable with informal, stream-of-consciousness writing. Although the range of writing abilities is broad, we find it generally true that students with more proficient writing skills fare better in their education courses, as well as in college and graduate studies. Given this reality, and in light of national statistics, we have spent many years reflecting on how to improve our teaching practices in order to support our students in becoming better writers.

We suggest that the PK-12 students in our country's schools need teachers who are great writers, who are familiar with the writing process, and who are willing to experience the process as writers. One way to teach excellent writing habits to students is to model excellent writing habits as educators (Gillespie, 1985; Morgan, 2010). Furthermore, Peter Elbow (1998), one of the great champions of the writing process, argued that all writers need to experience a variety of methods of writing in order to find tools that work for each individual. As professors in education, we have found that students enter our classes with a preconceived notion of writing as something they do as an assignment. Perhaps this perception stems from students' prior experiences with writing as a school-based task and/or the fact that writing is not generally taught as a stand-alone education course; unlike content areas, such as science, math, English, and social studies (and related methods courses), which are given specific airtime in programs of teacher education, the *art* of writing for educators typically is not.

Here we call attention to our distinction in language: *writing as educators* is generally not taught in teacher education, though classes, such as *teaching writing* or *writing methods,* are more likely to be included in a program of study. This might be because it is assumed that writing is explored within each content area, but we argue the following: Because writing is so critically important to school and life success, and because our nation does so poorly on standardized measures of writing proficiency, teachers and teacher candidates benefit from learning how to develop and strengthen their own writing. Furthermore, teachers modelling such writing practices can motivate and support students regardless of the grade or subject.

In this chapter, we explore techniques and strategies that will help you develop your writing skills as a teacher or teacher candidate. Just as there might be certain methods that you believe are quite effective at augmenting student understanding in a particular lesson, we contend that there are certain strategies that you can draw upon as a teacher to enhance your own writing about teaching and learning. In this chapter, we ask you to consider how the strategies and exercises might strengthen your writing as an educator. However, no singular strategy will work for all writers at all times, and meaningful teaching and learning does not follow a one-size-fits-all approach. Thus, it can be quite helpful to have a menu of options from which to choose when faced with a writing task. We envision the options presented in this chapter as choices that you might want to add to your menu.

In this chapter we discuss how to use writing to highlight, support, and promote your pedagogical choices. The Featured Assignment explores how to use writing as a means to consider and comment on teaching and learning, particularly in light of teacher performance assessments. While there are many books for educators on how to teach writing to PK-12 students, there are few resources on how educators, themselves, can use writing to demonstrate the strength of their pedagogy. This chapter begins the conversation on how the art of writing for educators can be leveraged as a tool for showcasing the power of your teaching.

DEVELOPING ROBUST WRITING

We believe that it is important for educators to model excellent writing by being excellent writers themselves. To that end, we open this section by exploring two techniques that teachers and teacher candidates can use to strengthen their writing. The first technique is to gather multiple sources of evidence, and the second is to engage in peer review. As you read about these strategies, consider setting aside time to try them and to write about your experiences. This kind of reflective writing will help you evaluate the impact of that particular strategy on your growth as a writer, and it will also prepare you for the material you will encounter in Chapter 4 of this book.

Gathering Multiple Sources of Evidence

Just as in any other piece of writing, one way to advance your argument is to offer multiple sources of evidence to support your claim. When one learns how to write literary essays in a middle or high school English class, this typically takes the form of advancing a thesis with three examples from the text to support the claim. These types of essays can feel formulaic, as young writers are often taught how to do this standard five-paragraph essay before branching out into other forms of expository writing. We want to encourage you to think beyond structures (such as the five-paragraph essay) that you might associate with writing already, and begin to look more broadly at how to make meaning through text. As you consider how to write about your teaching, you will also want to draw from salient examples in order to exemplify your points. These examples can come from multiple sources in and around your classroom and your teaching.

For example, as a 9th grade science teacher, you might want to persuade your school's administration to support you in partnering with colleagues in English and Social Studies to create a cross-curricular unit on climate change. In order to advocate for the shared planning time and/or extra resources that this endeavor would need, you will want to offer a sound and convincing rationale for your proposed project. Perhaps the most professional way to get your principal's attention about your new proposal is to write a letter that explains your position and advocates for your project. To do so, you need to gather multiple sources of evidence to support the claims that: (a) this cross-curricular unit is needed in order to engage students in critical thinking about the topic; (b) cross-curricular work has been shown to increase student success and retention of the material being presented; (c) quality cross-curricular work requires common planning time and resources; and (d) you have the ability to create and implement this unit well. Sources of evidence might include, but are not limited to:

- Appropriate grade-level standards that justify the objectives for this unit (cf. the Common Core State Standards and/or the learning standards adopted by your state, your district, or even your school).
- An academic article on cross-curricular work and its relative success in the classroom, as well as the supports (e.g., common planning time) necessary for such success.
- A practitioner-based article from an education weekly or quarterly publication that showcases a cross-curricular unit and its concomitant outcomes.
- A letter of support from guardians/caregivers who are eager to see their children engaged with cross-curricular work.
- A sample of student work from a prior lesson or unit that featured cross-curricular themes to show that you are familiar with the desired outcomes.
- A rubric that will be used to assess the final piece of student work.

Curriculum Matters: Power in Diverse Representations

A point we addressed in the Introduction and that we would like to revisit here is that no text is neutral. All texts render certain ideas more important than others. All texts display power to some extent, and all texts privilege certain pieces of evidence more than others. What this means is that the work you create as a writer will not be neutral. It will privilege the information that you seek to share. It will position certain activities or ideas as more important than others. For instance, in the previous example of a cross-curricular unit addressing climate change, you would be inherently positioning cross-curricular instruction as more important or effective than siloed, strictly discipline-specific instruction.

Even the process of gathering multiple sources of evidence has material consequences: which sources of evidence will you choose? Which will you omit? If you are citing research and scholarship, do the authors you cite represent diverse backgrounds and positions? If you are using student work, have you used work from students representing different abilities, races, genders, ethnicities and work styles? Answering these questions can help you position your work more strongly because you will acknowledge the ways in which the writing you put forth privileges and positions certain ideas.

To illustrate how to gather multiple sources of evidence in a convincing piece of writing, we provide an example of writing that was generously shared by one of the students in our course, *The Art of Writing for Educators*.[1] This *Letter to an Administrator*, designed for a hypothetical audience, illustrates how the teacher candidate combined topics in math and English Language Arts to create an engaging cross-curricular unit that augmented student learning. As you read the letter, please note a few key points. First, the author wrote a brief and compelling rationale for her work in the classroom. This is another way of saying that, overall, this piece is short enough to be appropriate for a busy administrator. We advise keeping your communications with your administration brief and meaningful. Principals are very busy with much to read and do throughout the day. A one-page single-spaced letter is an appropriate length for matters similar to this. Second, the author used Common Core State Standards as well as professional research to support her claims about connecting math and English Language Arts in a cross-curricular set of lessons. Third, the author conveyed her ideas with rich detail throughout her rationale, enabling us to visualize her lesson in illustrative ways. Pay attention to these three key features as you read the letter and our evaluative comments that follow.

Example of Student Work: Letter to an Administrator

Dear Principal Jones,

I am writing this letter to inform you of an activity I completed with my 7th grade math class. The goal of the activity was to have students describe two-dimensional shapes that are created in cross sections— also known as plane sections—of three-dimensional shapes when they are cut. Students modelled cubes of Play-Doh© and were challenged to create specific shapes in the cross section of the cube such as triangles and squares. Students were given a chart that asked specific questions about their experiment to promote critical thinking and provided space for students to record their observations. This is a unique activity because while students were focused on math, the chart allowed them to practice their writing skills by guiding the students to describe their discoveries.

The activity included the use of manipulatives and writing in math, both of which help students to comprehend the material being taught. There are several articles that support this claim:

- Manipulatives can create a positive learning environment that encourages student engagement, allows students to better understand mathematical concepts, and supports complex mathematical thinking (Cockett & Kilgour, 2015).
- Through different types of mathematical writing, students can be engaged in unique ways that allow them to better interpret and reflect on their work (Colonnese et al., 2018).

Manipulatives can create an enjoyable learning environment. For instance, while the students waited to receive Play-Doh©, they were smiling and intently staring at the containers. When the students were prompted to begin the activity, they eagerly ripped off the lids, grabbed the dental floss, and started making cuts. This shows that this is a fun activity that visually supported their understanding of cross sections.

Students also engaged in mathematical writing which helps enhance their learning experience. For example, the chart directed students to make two cuts parallel to the base of the cube, then describe the cross sections. One student recorded the following: "All cuts parallel to the base will have a cross section of a square because all sides of a cube are equal." This application of academic vocabulary exhibits an understanding of several aspects of math. Taken together, the research and my observations from this lesson suggest that a mathematical investigation along with a writing component encourage students' learning through the use of a cross-disciplinary activity.

This activity satisfies the following math and writing Common Core Learning Standards:

- CCSS.Math.Content.7.G.3.: Describe the two-dimensional figures that result from slicing three-dimensional figures, as in plane sections of right rectangular prisms and right rectangular pyramids.
- CCSS.ELA-Literacy.7.W.2.a.: Introduce a topic clearly, previewing what is to follow; organize ideas, concepts, and information, using strategies such as definition, classification, comparison/contrast, and cause/effect; include formatting (e.g., headings), graphics (e.g., charts, tables), and multimedia when useful to aiding comprehension.

The activity is in accordance with these standards for several reasons. My students actively used their hands to cut the Play-Doh© cube and create a 2D figure in the cross section. The students were able to evaluate the shapes in the cross section they created. While students compared and contrasted their recorded observations from the chart, students gasped when they realized they had to cut through as many faces of the cube as there were sides of the shape that was created in the cross section (e.g., 3 faces for a triangle). These standards served as a guide for students and supported the cross-disciplinary nature of the activity.

This activity was exciting for students while adhering to Common Core Learning Standards. This shows that learning can be fun. Hands-on experiences and visuals create an enjoyable environment and aid in the students' understanding of the lesson. The use of writing in math encourages students to develop ideas, reflect on their work, and internalize information. Based on this, I believe all math teachers should use manipulatives and writing in their classrooms to promote student success and a positive learning environment. I would welcome the opportunity to discuss this further!

Sincerely,
Classroom Teacher

Evaluating the Letter to an Administrator

Now that you have read the sample letter, please reflect on the strength of the author's writing by responding to the following questions:

- What sources of evidence did this author use to support her claim?
- What stands out to you as particularly convincing?
- What can you take from this letter and apply to your own content area?
- If you were taking the position of an administrator, would this letter satisfy you? Why or why not?

From our perspective as professors, we are struck by a few compelling features. First, the writer clearly communicated the strength of this approach in the opening paragraph (e.g., she states that this unique activity enabled her students to explore a math concept and use their writing skills). Second, the writer called upon existing academic resources to provide further evidence for her claim that this activity enhanced student learning. The author referenced the academic texts in clear and convincing language and used standards from two different disciplines to illustrate how this practice bridges content areas.

Third, the writer used specific phrases and examples throughout the letter to show her reader the value of the activity (rather than tell her reader). For example, she wrote, "When the students were prompted to begin the activity, they eagerly ripped off the lids, grabbed the dental floss, and started making cuts." This descriptive sentence allows us, as readers, to see the excitement and enthusiasm that the students displayed. It is far more effective to show this with details than to write something akin to, "My students were excited to begin this new lesson." As professors, we advocate using strategies that show rather than tell throughout any piece of writing. These strategies include using examples, replacing adjectives (e.g., motivating) with descriptive details (e.g., "students eagerly ripped off the lids"), and including phrases and sentences that describe movement, actions, or behaviors. We encourage you to try these techniques throughout your writing.

Engaging in a Writing Workshop or Peer Review

The process of peer review, or what is commonly known as *writing workshop* in PK-12 classrooms, can be useful to teachers as well. Just like students, educators need time and space to process their thoughts, receive feedback, create revisions, and adjust final drafts. In a PK-12 classroom, the writing process usually follows a set series of steps:

- Brainstorming a set of ideas for a given topic using a variety of different types of graphic organizers
- Organizing those ideas into a sequence for a written piece
- Drafting an initial iteration of the piece
- Revising via peer review or a writing workshop
- Finalizing a finished product

Peer interaction might be a hallmark of the revision stage, but it also is an essential component to all five steps. Brainstorming informally or formally with colleagues can help set a thought in motion. Likewise, when thinking about how to organize the sequence for a written piece, reviewing the ideas with a colleague can be helpful, especially if you are concerned about going off on a tangent. Drafting, revising, and finalizing all involve the completion of a written piece with and through the feedback of others.

Curriculum Matters: The Writing Process

Before going any further about the writing process, we would like to call your attention here to larger theories that have circulated around rhetoric and composition. While countless scholars have weighed in on numerous debates surrounding the composition of written texts, we pick up this discussion with Peter Elbow's work to give you a brief overview of some of the larger trajectories in the field. In contrast to a stricter adherence to formulaic writing (such as a five-paragraph essay that is written for a college course without consideration of audience or voice), Peter Elbow argued that writing is a process, and, in fact, he privileged the process of writing over the final written product. Elbow's (1998) work highlighted the importance of expression and discovery as writers craft their pieces, with a particular emphasis on writers finding their voice as they work through iterative cycles of a writing process.

Linda Flower and John Hayes (1981) argued that writing is not a linear process that can be reduced to prewriting, writing, and editing/revising. Instead, they suggested that there is a much more complex series of decisions that flow back and forth among various stages of composing text while a writer is writing. They called this model *the cognitive process theory of writing*, and their work is distinguished by a focus on the cognitive faculties that are at play in the process of writing.

From there, we call attention to a turn towards a critical orientation and examination of writing and the writing process. Within the last few decades, there has been a move away from the transmission model—an approach to learning that is based on the teacher holding the knowledge and transmitting it to students—to a student-driven one wherein students are agents of their own discoveries. Scholars such as Paolo Freire (1972), bell hooks (2014) and Lisa Delpit (2006) have focused a lens on a critical and transformative approach to pedagogy that they argue is needed in order to create interactive classrooms in which all children are involved in creating knowledge and meaning. This is an important shift from earlier work on writing and meaning making, one that focuses on critical transformation. We call attention to these important trends in teaching and learning about writing so that you, the reader, can situate yourself and your learning within the larger trajectory of the field.

Peer interaction and transformative practices can take place in the writing workshop, a generative environment in the classroom where students are both working on writing skills and gaining confidence as writers (Fletcher & Portalupi, 2001). Depending on the context of the classroom environment, an effective writing workshop might consist of students participating in a significant amount of writing and experiencing failure and setbacks with their writing (e.g., "false starts, blank pages, misspellings, and so on" (Fletcher & Portalupi, 2001, p. 5)). Additionally, the writing workshop serves as a time wherein the student-writer confers with a peer and/or a teacher in order to discuss the work at hand. These sessions are typically guided by reflective questions such as: I am confused by what _____ means. What can you do to make this part clearer? Or, are you ready to try _____ (figurative language, dialogue, descriptive opening, etc.)?

Setting up a writing workshop for you as an educator is one way to build in time for reflection and gain insight from a trusted colleague/peer. We encourage you to experiment with a writing workshop by reviewing a piece of writing with a colleague or peer. Suggestions for your review include, but are not limited to: a letter to an administrator; a letter to families; an assignment description and rubric; an article for an education journal; a grant proposal; materials for certification or National Board Certification; or a lesson plan. Although we fully recognize the realities of scheduling and curricular constraints, we believe that the benefits of dedicating time and space to peer review are well worth the effort.

Curriculum Matters: Exploring Peer Review

Grab a colleague and a piece of writing and try out a writing workshop or peer review. Each person spends a designated number of minutes reading the other's work. Then, take turns providing feedback, using the following guiding questions to facilitate conversation about your writing sample:

1. Point out a specific phrase, sentence, or passage of your partner's writing that was especially clear to you as a reader. Tell your partner what you understood from that portion of writing.
2. Point out a specific phrase, sentence or passage where your partner's writing is confusing or less clear. Ask your partner to talk about the idea out loud and take notes while you listen to your partner talk. Evaluate your written notes together and see if you can find an idea for a revision for that portion of writing.

Concluding Thoughts on Developing Robust Writing

In this section we explored two possible methods for rationalizing your pedagogy through writing: gathering multiple sources of evidence to support your claims and engaging in a writing workshop or peer review to improve your writing. We highlight these two techniques in particular because we believe—to borrow a term from the esteemed math educator, Jo Boaler (2015)—that they are *low floor and high ceiling*. The entry points for these two methods have a *low floor*, meaning that everyone can attempt these strategies and there are no special skill sets you need in order to try them out. Similarly, these strategies have a *high ceiling*, meaning that the outcomes can soar as high as you want them to be. You can continue working on gathering *just right* sources of evidence and soliciting feedback from colleagues without having a natural stopping point. You, as the writer, determine where the ceiling is and where it could be.

In order to further your endeavors when writing about teaching, you can also expose yourself to a wide array of writing in education. One way to grow as a writer, in particular with education content, is to explore the variety of texts that exist. As a teacher or teacher candidate, you likely have come across textbooks and articles in your education classes or professional development sessions that present writing about teaching. These are great tools for exploring foundations and theories of education. Adding on, you can investigate a number of print and online resources for evaluating educational tools, structures, and trends. Some websites we recommend are Edutopia (www.edutopia.org) and Project Zero (www.pz.harvard.edu). These websites curate articles and videos on a variety of topics related to PK-12 education, including both general topics and content-specific ones.

Another suggestion is to follow the Education columns in major newspapers or magazines. These reports include current trends and issues in education, ranging from legislative policy to individual school reforms. *The New York Times* (www.nytimes.com), *The Washington Post* (www.thewashingtonpost.com), and *The Wall Street Journal* (www.wsj.com) offer a range of articles on education issues that face the nation at large. Similarly, the National Education Association produces a quarterly magazine titled *NEA Today* that explores challenging teaching questions and solutions (www.nea.org).

Furthermore, you can join an education organization that fits your interest and content area. These organizations provide a rich and expansive way to get more familiar with content and valued teaching strategies in your area of expertise. The following list of education organizations is just one way to get started with more content-specific writing to broaden your expertise:

- *Math*: National Council of Teachers of Mathematics (www.nctm.org). They provide a number of journals to their members, covering a wide range of topics in math instruction.
- *English*: National Council of Teachers of English (www.ncte.org). With a large number of print and online journals, chronicles, and newsletters, NCTE offers a rich assortment of writing about English instruction.
- *Social Studies*: National Council for the Social Studies (www.socialstudies.org). They have journals dedicated to teaching and learning in the field of social studies.
- *Science*: National Science Teachers Association (www.nsta.org). There are five NSTA journals, all of which offer engaging and timely explorations of science teaching.

- *Writing*: National Writing Project (www.nwp.org). The National Writing Project offers a plethora of resources from print journals to books to newsletters. All publications are geared towards helping teachers develop their students as writers *and* develop as writers themselves.
- *The Arts*: Excellent writing about education in the arts can be found in places like the National Art Education Association (www.arteducators. org) or the Music Teachers National Association (www.mtna.org).

After you have perused a number of print resources, another way to develop as a writer is to curate a set of mentor texts in your field. In the context of this book, a mentor text is any piece of writing (e.g., book, journal article, blog post) that exemplifies particular writing strategies, tools, or methods. A mentor text serves as an exemplar, something to which you can turn when you are looking for models and examples of excellent writing. You can find mentor texts in a variety of places. When we were writing our dissertations, we each found an exemplary dissertation from a former doctoral student, and that work served as a mentor text for our own writing. As academics, we find that scholarly articles in our fields serve as mentor texts in our current settings. We each still use mentor texts on a regular basis.

The mentor text is important because it is an example of good writing in your discipline. Writing is hard. Even with clear assignment expectations, well-crafted rubrics, and explicit guidelines, writing tasks can be confusing. Often the most effective move is to *show* writers what good writing looks like in addition to explaining it to them. The same goes for our students in PK-12 classrooms. Mentor texts—alongside clear expectations and rubrics—are a strong way of establishing good writing habits and eliciting the best writing from our students. Ultimately, the point of mentor texts is to enhance the writing process by reading texts in that same genre. To that end, we suggest the book *Teaching Matters* by Beverly Falk and Megan Blumenreich (2012) as an excellent compilation of practitioner-written reflections about classrooms and teaching. Beyond being engaging and enjoyable to read, the practitioner contributions in this book illustrate what excellent reflective writing can look like in the field of education.

WRITING TO SHOWCASE PEDAGOGY

There is no single set of writing practices to be used to the exclusion of all others, but there are some common habits and routines that can work well in PK-12 classrooms. In the previous section, we explored what some of those strategies are as they relate to *your writing* as an educator. In this section, we focus on how to showcase the strengths of your *teaching* in and through your writing. For example, you might want to communicate about classroom activities with your students' families. Or you might want to write about the benefits of an exchange program in which your students recently participated. To communicate with others about these pedagogical choices, you will need to draw upon your writing skills to highlight the strengths of these curricular units, routines, and/or teaching methods. In the section that follows we explore different types of writing that can showcase your teaching.

Teaching Statement

A teaching statement (also called a teaching philosophy) is an opportunity to draw attention to your strengths as a teacher and explain to your current and potential employers why you would be an asset to their school community. It is an opportunity to showcase your pedagogy and illustrate the type of classroom environment that you believe is most educative for children. Stephen Brookfield (2015) talks about a philosophy of teaching in the following way: "Teaching is about making some kind of dent in the world so that the world is different than it was before you practiced your craft" (p. 18). An exceptional teaching statement highlights the moves and strategies that you employ to make "some kind of dent."

You can leverage your teaching statement to underscore how you will create an educational environment in which diverse students can learn and thrive. Additionally, you can use the teaching statement to illustrate your ability to adapt to the learning needs of your individual students *and* your class(es) overall. Whereas some on-site interviews for prospective teaching positions might include a demonstration lesson, some might not. Through showing, not telling, your teaching statement can serve as an illustrative way for a prospective administrator to "see" you in the classroom, especially if you do not have the chance to demonstrate your teaching during an interview. Highlighting what you do exceptionally well as an educator communicates what you believe about teaching and learning, how you envision moving a diverse group of students towards your shared goals, and what you will do to create a learning environment that stimulates everyone.

Practitioner Journal/Teaching Reflection

A diary-like, personal practitioner journal or a teaching reflection is a great way to keep track of your thoughts on classroom practices and generate ideas for growth. Many professionals track their work in some form, through a pocket notebook, a series of voice memos, scribbles throughout the house, and other informal ways. Whatever your preference, we recommend making a daily or weekly practice of recording your thoughts and reflections. Start with an evaluation of strengths: What went well in today's lesson? In what ways did students show engagement? How did students show mastery of the skills and content? From there, move on to reflections that consider growth and improvement: What did not go well in today's lesson? Where were the gaps in student understanding? What resources might prove more useful in getting content across to the students in subsequent lessons?

Accumulating and revisiting reflections over time can have a positive impact on one's teaching practice. Not only does it create space and time for thought, it can serve as a catalyst for action as well. In addition to offering an opportunity to look inward, reflections can serve as a basis for future communication about teaching practices with colleagues, administrators, and other stakeholders.

Communicating with Stakeholders

Frequently, you will be asked to communicate with stakeholders about your teaching practices. Stakeholders include, but are not limited to, students, guardians, family members, administrators, curriculum specialists, and professional development providers. These communications can take a variety of forms—your principal might ask you for a teaching reflection, or you might choose to write about an innovative unit to share your knowledge with colleagues. The following example of teacher writing showcases one such type of communication. It was generously shared with us from a student in our course. As you read the letter, take note of the strategies the writer uses to construct an engaging and well-rounded letter that communicates the value of her teaching to her students' families.

Example of Student Work: Letter to Families

Dear Families,

I am writing a letter home to let the guardians of my students understand the type of approach I am taking during my lessons at your child's school. As an educator, I believe it is of the utmost importance to place a heavy emphasis on writing, especially for students at this stage of their academic career. As a Spanish teacher, I also find writing to be an excellent approach to learning and comprehending a foreign language. Students will strengthen their academic writing in the Spanish language by incorporating vocabulary that they learn in my lessons. In my class, I have also made it a point to incorporate various subjects other than Spanish into the writing curriculum. For example, your child has recently completed an assignment constructed between the Spanish department and the history department. This assignment tasked my students with writing a fictional letter in the Spanish language from the viewpoint of a prominent historical figure involved in historical events in Latin America. This assignment is a true example of cross-curricular writing because students needed to draw on historical facts while also maintaining a cohesive flow of writing in the Spanish language.

As a teacher in a school within New York State, I am required to create lessons that fulfill the Common Core Standards for each subject. I have chosen two Common Core Standards that are related to the cross-disciplinary assignment mentioned in the previous paragraph. The first standard requires the writing within the assignment to captivate the reader and produce words that create a sense of imagery. This standard mentions the use of clear word choice and expressive details to help the reader to understand the point of view of the writer. In the "Latin American Letter Assignment," students were required to use sensory language and illustrative details to paint a picture to their reader. I asked my students to be as descriptive as possible, feeding on their knowledge from their World History lessons regarding the subject. The second standard that coincides with the learning objectives of this lesson is one that concerns writing narratives. The language used in this standard requires students to create a real or imagined narrative using pertinent details, written with a cohesive flow of thoughts. Students in my class were asked to create a narrative of this nature when writing their imagined letters from prominent Latin American figures. Students were required to base their letter on a major historical event that occurred in the life of a prominent Latin American figure. When writing this letter, students were required to create a narrative with important events presented in correct sequential order.

I truly hope that the rest of the school year brings opportunities for your children to create pieces of writing that transcend the traditional boundaries of subjects. I will do my best to make sure that your child is a well-rounded writer by the time we break for summer. It is assignments like the "Latin American Letter Assignment" that truly bridge the content of two subject areas. If you should have any questions about my approach regarding my lesson structure or if you would like to discuss a particular assignment, please feel free to contact me. I am always willing to meet with parents after school to discuss the learning occurring daily in my classroom.

Sincerely,
Classroom Teacher

Evaluating the Letter to Families

Once you have read the student sample, please reflect on the strength of the student's writing vis-à-vis the following questions:

- In what ways does this author convey the strength of her teaching?
- How does the author communicate the strength of the learning environment?
- What can you take from this letter and apply to your own practice?

As we evaluate this piece of student writing, there are a few compelling features that warrant further attention. First, the writer offers specific details regarding the Spanish content as well as the History content. It is clear to the reader that the students will be using their Spanish language skills from the viewpoint of a prominent historical figure (e.g., "This assignment tasked my students with writing a fictional letter in the Spanish language from the viewpoint of a prominent historical figure involved in historical events in Latin America."). The author gives a clear summary of how two content areas will be used to generate new learning.

Second, the writer creates a compelling case for how this lesson satisfies state-designated learning standards *and* she puts these standards in clear language that is accessible to students' families. Take note of the second paragraph in which the author introduces the state standards, narrates them in easy-to-understand language, and *makes a clear connection between the assignment and the standards*. Third, the author generates enthusiasm for this lesson and clearly explains how the students' writing will be developed as a result of this lesson. The author explains that this assignment will bridge two content areas and offers a warm invitation for further discussion to families and caregivers who might wish to contact the teacher regarding this lesson.

Curriculum Matters: Audience Awareness

Please note the need to adjust voice and tone when writing to different audiences in education. Whereas you likely would use field-specific language (e.g., metacognition, constructivism, cross-literate practices) and cite scholars in the field to support your claims when writing to an administrator, the tone you use to address families should be professional and courteous without being overly academic or obtuse. You also might need to provide families with some brief explanation or context for certain types of approaches to instruction (e.g., do not assume they are familiar with the approach). For instance, in the sample Letter to Families, the writer incorporated an overview of cross-curricular writing when describing her assignment rather than assuming the reader would know the meaning of this phrase. Additionally, you might be required to translate notices sent home to families, or you might need to avail yourself of translation services offered by your school.

Concluding Thoughts on Writing to Showcase Pedagogy

The strategies and examples that we introduced in this section provide options for tools that showcase the strength of your pedagogical choices. There are plenty of times that this will be required of you, and, in those times, you will likely want to express the value and power of your teaching in clear, concise language.

FEATURED ASSIGNMENT: COMMENTING ON
TEACHING AND LEARNING

The Featured Assignment for this chapter draws on multiple frameworks: writing about teaching, standardized performance assessments for teaching, and evaluation tools for assessing writing about teaching. The sample commentaries that we include offer a unique opportunity to analyze writing about teaching and learning in a way that is aligned with (but not specifically taught to) the edTPA exam. Teachers and teacher candidates who are interested in developing these can use the analysis opportunities presented in this section to strengthen their own writing. The directions and samples in this Featured Assignment offer a detailed look at student work that is aligned with the parameters of edTPA; however, we believe that these samples also would be helpful in preparing a wide variety of teacher assessments. In this way, we anticipate that these samples will serve as useful tools for writing about teaching in generative ways *and* for preparing to write a comprehensive performance assessment.

We chose to highlight this particular assignment because it affords the reader the opportunity to:

- Evaluate one tool for commenting on teaching and learning.
- Analyze one sample commentary on teaching and learning practices.
- Apply the skills gained from writing commentaries across teaching contexts.
- Reflect on tasks associated with standardized performance assessments for teaching.

The directions for this Featured Assignment are as follows: This assignment affords you the opportunity to examine and explain educational pedagogy and practice. You will be examining teaching through the eyes of a teacher to help you think about the art of teaching in relation to objectives, goals, activities, and feedback. In so doing, you will consider how a lesson is guided by its objectives and how a lesson demonstrates evidence of student progress. You will then be asked to communicate this information in a written commentary in order to help you hone your skills in this writing context.

More specifically, you will watch a sample video of an educator in the classroom. Watching the video, you will take notes on the teaching practices used and evidence of student engagement. Your notes will help you construct your written commentary in which you assume the role of the teacher in the video and respond to the prompts as if you delivered the instruction yourself.

The video used for this assignment is part of the Annenberg Foundation's educational video library repository, which encompasses many teaching examples. All of the Annenberg Foundation's resources can be found at www.learner.org.[2] Although we recognize that, in years to come, these links might no longer be stable, we have found the Annenberg site to be particularly reliable throughout our teaching careers. Additionally, we take this opportunity to advocate for an established repository of videos that educators can use to evaluate strong teaching in a variety of educational contexts. Teacher candidates and teacher educators can benefit from a set of videos that support the development of writing in education through evaluation of practice.

After watching the video for this assignment, you will craft a written commentary in which you respond to the following four prompts as though you were the educator teaching the class:

1. Explain how your instruction engaged students in developing essential knowledge and/or requisite skills.
2. Describe how, if at all, the instruction drew upon students' prior academic learning and personal, cultural, and community assets to support new learning.
3. Explain how you elicited student responses and provided feedback to (a) promote critical thinking, and (b) use requisite knowledge and/or skills to comprehend or complete a task.
4. Explain how you supported students' application of content area knowledge, vocabulary, and skills in a meaningful way.

Additionally, as you write your commentary, you will highlight content-area vocabulary as well as academic language.[3] When you prepare a portfolio for the edTPA, you will need to explore the academic language demands of your lessons. That is, to what extent are you teaching vocabulary words, syntax structures, and discourse patterns that are specific to (and appropriate for) your content and grade level?

In consideration of this requirement of the edTPA, in this commentary we ask you to demonstrate proper usage of at least four academic language words and at least four content-area vocabulary words. Put simply, academic language includes words that students need to know in order to understand objectives and complete instructional aims. These words identify a particular kind of thinking or engagement in schools. Examples of academic vocabulary words include: explaining, narrating, persuading and synthesizing. Unlike academic language, content-area vocabulary words are specific to the particular discipline. Some examples of content-area vocabulary include: beaker, temperature, gravity (science); latitude, longitude, border (social studies); equation, theorem, equilateral (math); thesis, metaphor, explication (English). In this assignment you will use four academic language words and four content-area vocabulary words in appropriate and generative ways in your commentary. The objective of this portion of the assignment is to work with higher-level vocabulary words in order to strengthen your writing.

Evaluating Sample Student Work

This section features work from a student who has taken our course, *The Art of Writing for Educators*. The student responded to the commentary prompts after watching a video that features a high school English teacher working with her students on spoken word poetry. More specifically, the teacher and her students analyzed the poetry of *griots*, a kind of poet or storyteller who maintains a tradition of oral history in West Africa. The English teacher's lesson created room for the students to evaluate how modern-day musicians and rappers could also be seen as *griots* and provided space for her students to create poems that mirrored this tradition of oral storytelling. We provide this student's commentary responses as a way for you to reflect upon and evaluate this particular form of rationalizing pedagogy. As you read the student's commentary responses (recalling that she is writing from the perspective of the teacher in the video), consider the evaluation questions that follow and use them to assess this mentor text. Also note that these commentary prompts can be applied to any segment of teacher practice, offering multiple and repeated opportunities to reflect on teaching and learning.

Commentary Prompt #1: Explain how your instruction engaged students in developing essential knowledge and/or requisite skills.

In the beginning of the class, I wrote the learning objective on the board and provided students with two prompting questions, "What is a griot?" and "What is oral tradition?" This gave the students some insight into what we'd be learning about in this workshop, with a clear learning intention. I did not define the word "griot" for my students, but instead allowed them to respond with their own understanding, on which I elaborated. The intention of this was so the students would be engaged in learning the content, rather than being told the answers. I judged the depth of the students' responses and explanations in our big group discussion to determine if the students had grasped the content knowledge. For example, one student said: "We're all griots and the way that we dress, our style... all of that tells a story." This comment depicted this student's lucid understanding. I chose to dedicate a large amount of time to this discussion as it allowed all my students a chance to contribute and describe their ideas, making them active learners. If students did not volunteer to contribute, I would call upon them, for example, when I said, "add to that a little bit more Leah." This meant that students had to pay attention and always be thinking, rather than zone out. Furthermore, by making this lesson relevant to my students, I am encouraging them to develop content knowledge by choice, outside of class time. This reflected their engagement in the task as they wanted to locate more information.

Evaluating Commentary Prompt #1:

As you evaluate the student response, pay attention to how well the author uses specific, accurate, and relevant descriptions/examples to support her claims. Additionally, find places where the author *shows* how the teacher in the video draws on prior knowledge, develops new knowledge, and extends students' skill sets in the lesson. We see strengths in the following areas of this prompt response:

- The author describes *how* she set the learning objective by providing the specific questions used to stimulate the students' thinking.
- The author explains *why* she did not define the word griot and what her pedagogical reasoning was for that particular move.
- When explaining *how* she assessed whether the students were developing new knowledge, the author includes specific student quotes and details from the classroom.

Commentary Prompt #2: Describe how, if at all, the instruction drew upon students' prior academic learning and personal, cultural, and community assets with new learning.

To draw on students' personal assets, I asked "Who would be considered griots today, in our society?" Their responses were personal and relatable to their own world. For example, one student answered that "rappers" are griots, followed by another student who built on this answer. I connected my students to the topic on a personal level by explaining that "everyone in here is in griot training." This makes the learning more inclusive for each individual. Furthermore, I attempted to make the study of poetry relatable to the students by using a rap song, which drew on many of my student's interests. This particular rap song focused on the subway, a familiar mode of transport for these students of New York. Students were able to use their prior knowledge of metaphors to interpret the subway with a deeper meaning of going on a journey. They unpacked the complexity of this rap by linking it to racial and cultural themes. For example, one student stated that the meaning behind the rap was "a representation of a journey back to Africa, his home." This makes the learning more relevant and engaging for them.

Evaluating Commentary Prompt #2:

In this portion of the author's commentary, she provides a clear and compelling analysis for how she addresses cultural assets and links those assets to the students' personal and prior knowledge. Again, in this response, we see the author using language that *shows* us (rather than *tells* us) what the students in the classroom did. For example, the author suggests that the connection between the topic and the students' personal lives was evident in the statement she made about everyone being in "griot training." Further, she explains that the rap song she used and the particular context of that song (e.g., subway) were deliberate choices because of their personal connection to the students' lives. Additionally, we see strength in the following attributes of this prompt response:

- The author uses specific content-area vocabulary in this response such as *metaphors*, as well as academic language such as *interpret*. The use of academic language and content specific vocabulary creates a response that is detailed and professional.
- The author pulls relevant quotes from the students in the classroom to illustrate how they are making connections among the content of the lesson, their prior knowledge, and their cultural histories.

Commentary Prompt #3: Explain how you elicited student responses and provided feedback to promote critical thinking and use requisite knowledge and/or skills to comprehend or complete a task.

During classroom discussion, I made an effort to involve all my students in the conversation, rather than have one or two students dominating the discussion. This ensures that all students are involved in analyzing the poem and providing their own perspective. I always provided a comment after each student response, in order to validate and extend their ideas. An example of this was when a student made relevant and quality points about "the man" but I wanted to expand on this, therefore I added "Ok what's going on in the poem, who is the man that they're referring to?" This ensured that the students were pushed to examine the poem and promote critical thinking. Furthermore, when completing their writing task, I chose to put students into groups to allow them to "gel together" and "connect when talking about really important issues." The reason for this was so students could collaborate with each other, building on each other's ideas about these issues, in order to come up with the best quality final product. By conducting this activity in small groups, I created a classroom climate in which all students were expected to contribute. The next day, students were given the opportunity to present their small-group work to the class, including to our guest visitor Abiodun Oyewole. Mr. Oyewole was the author of the spoken word poem "On the Subway" that we had listened to in a prior class. The presence of this "real life" poet gave students the opportunity to get feedback on their work from a respected poet and author. This kind of feedback made my students feel acknowledged and appreciated.

Evaluating Commentary Prompt #3:

In this portion of the commentary, the objective is to provide specific, accurate, and relevant descriptions and examples of how the teacher uses feedback to promote critical thinking and guide student learning. We see strengths in the author's response in the following three areas:

- The author shows us very concretely how she elicited more information from a student who initially provided a terse response. Rather than simply moving on from that student, the author followed up with another question that deepened the student's thinking, and she explains all of that with examples in her response.
- The author clearly explains her rationale for group work, stating what her intentions were with this pedagogical choice.
- The author ties her pedagogical choices to critical thinking at different points in this paragraph response. She explains how she believes those choices enhanced student learning and critical analysis.

Commentary Prompt #4: Explain how you supported students' application of content area knowledge, vocabulary, and skills in a meaningful way.

Throughout this class, we thoroughly unpacked the poem "On the Subway" and the key ideas associated with this. To support the knowledge students had gained in this content area, I had the author, Mr. Oyewole come and visit the class. When he asked, "What have y'all been learning about," the students were able to use their new understanding and vocabulary to showcase their knowledge. This was evident in the students' questions such as "Do you consider

> *yourself a griot?" This question shows that the student was able to articulate the vocabulary in context in a meaningful way. When the students presented the poems they created in their small groups, they used pertinent vocabulary and relevant metaphors. Not only were they applying their knowledge, vocabulary and skills, but they were passionate while doing so. From here, they were able to take on feedback from their personalized work to further enhance their skills. The discussion that students had with Mr. Oyewole allowed them to put their content knowledge and vocabulary in use. It gave their learning a purpose. By the end of this unit of work, I could see that they learned new language, which enhanced their vocabulary immensely.*

Evaluating Commentary Prompt #4:
This response provides specific, accurate, and relevant descriptions and examples of how the teacher supports the students' application of content area knowledge, vocabulary, and skills in a meaningful way. Although showing rather than telling would strengthen this response, the author begins to:

- Provide an example of a student using the content-specific vocabulary and detail the positive impacts that were made by the guest speaker.
- Illustrate how these pedagogical choices afforded students an opportunity to put their newly gained vocabulary to use in context.

CONCLUDING THOUGHTS: WRITING ABOUT TEACHING AND LEARNING

This chapter invited you to reflect on rationalizing your own pedagogical practices. Going back to the guiding questions at the beginning, we hope that—after reading this chapter—you feel more equipped to communicate about the practices you engage in as a teacher *and* illustrate the educational power of those practices. We invite you to do some of your own writing about teaching and then return to the examples we included in this chapter— the Letter to an Administrator, the Letter to Families, and the Commentary Responses—in order to reflect on your ability to provide specific, detailed narratives that *show* your excellent teaching rather than *tell* about it.

As you finish this chapter, consider the following questions to help you deepen your understanding and apply what you have learned.

Questions for Further Consideration

1. There are many ways to showcase your talents as an educator, and, among them, clear written communication is key. Over the course of your teaching career, you will craft letters to families and administrators, write insightful commentaries about your teaching, and highlight your strengths as an educator. Currently, what are your teaching strengths? Looking ahead, what pedagogical skills would you like to develop?

2. You will likely need to showcase your teaching practices in writing via some form of performance assessment as you seek professional certification. What are the licensing and certification standards/expectations in your state? How will these impact your path to the classroom? What steps might you take now to ensure success with these assessments?

NOTES

[1] Permission was obtained for all student work presented in this book. We have obscured the students' identities.

[2] The specific video referenced in the commentary can be found at the following link during the time of publication: https://www.learner.org/series/the-expanding-canon-teaching-multicultural-literature-in-high-school/critical-pedagogy-abiodun-oyewole-and-lawson-fusao-inada/. For search purposes within the Annenberg website, the title of this particular resource is "Critical Pedagogy: Abiodun Oyewole and Lawson Fusao Inada."

[3] The edTPA requires candidates to use academic language, or verbs that demonstrate students' active learning.

EXPANSIVE WRITING BEYOND CONTENT AND PAGE

GUIDING QUESTIONS

This chapter asks you to consider the different forms that writing might take within and across content areas (English, math, social studies, science, and so on). As you read this chapter, please consider the following guiding questions:

1. What type(s) of writing and communication do *you* regularly engage in every day? What type(s) of writing and communication might *your* current or future students engage in regularly? How might these form(s) of writing and communication influence the types of writing employed in your own classroom?
2. In what ways do you envision writing being part of lessons or courses that are not explicitly focused on reading and writing (i.e., non-English Language Arts settings)? How might different forms of writing enhance instruction in these settings?

INTRODUCTION

As you likely know from your education classes (or soon will), students across all grade levels are asked to communicate their thinking in a variety of disciplinary contexts. This practice in communication not only cuts across content areas (e.g., science and literacy), but also across form, as not all communication is solely based in alphabetic text. For example, math lessons might require students to communicate their thinking through equations, formulas, mathematical proofs, and problem solving. Likewise, students in science classes might collect various forms of data, create evidence-based arguments using a variety of data displays and representations, and communicate their ideas to an audience of their peers, teachers, families, and possibly others. As you will see in the examples provided in the *Curriculum Matters: Learning Standards* box that follows, students might communicate their ideas using cladograms (diagrams depicting relationships among organisms) in studies of evolutionary relationships in science, maps in social studies, visual fraction models in mathematics, and visual art works in art classes.

Curriculum Matters: Learning Standards

Loved or maligned, learning standards often play a substantial role in the types of content addressed in PK-12 classrooms. Although standards often provide guidance for what material should be addressed in specific content areas, they also can support teachers in thinking about curricular connections, especially with respect to writing and literacy. The following list contains examples of national and local standards that support writing in content areas other than English Language Arts, often employing different forms of writing as they do so.

- Students in a tenth-grade science class have been assigned a project in which they are asked to "communicate scientific information that common ancestry and biological evolution are supported by multiple lines of empirical evidence" (NGSS Lead States, 2013, HS-LS4-1).
- During a social studies unit titled "Geography, Humans, and the Environment," second grade students are asked to "create maps...that represent their classroom, school, or community, and maps that illustrate places in stories" (EngageNY.org of the New York State Department of Education, 2016, p. 34).
- Fifth grade students learning about fractions are asked to "solve real world problems involving multiplication of fractions and mixed numbers, e.g., by using visual fraction models or equations to represent the problem" (National Governors Association Center for Best Practices and Council of Chief State School Officers, 2010, CCSS. Math.Content.5.NF.B.6).
- Visual arts students in seventh grade are asked to "apply visual organizational strategies to design and produce a work of art, design, or media that clearly communicates information or ideas" (State Education Agency Directors of Arts Education, 2014, VA:Cr2.3.7a).

This is an excellent opportunity for you to think about curricular connections for your own current or future teaching. Locate one or two learning standards relevant to your content area, and consider the types of writing opportunities highlighted by these standards, as well as what other types of curricular connections they might support in the classroom by noting (a) the standard source; (b) the standard description; (c) writing connections; d) non-ELA curricular connections.

Often writing can be discipline-specific. A science lab report, for instance, is different from a book report, which is different from a biography of an historical figure. While simple, this example illustrates that, although students might write in a variety of classes, *how* they write (e.g., style, convention) and *what* they write can be markedly different. Instead of getting mired in the details of conventions in each discipline, we turn our attention to writing that is an integrated experience informed by experiences in and beyond the classroom. This chapter focuses on the different forms that writing can take, as well as ways that writing can be used across grade levels to create meaningful connections among content areas for your current and/ or future students. We conclude with a description of this chapter's Featured Assignment, which is a digital storytelling assignment designed to help you reflect upon and, hopefully, even challenge, your own notions of writing.

WRITING BEYOND THE ELA LESSON AND CLASSROOM

When asked in which content area the most writing takes place in PK-12 educational settings, one might expect most students, teachers, and teacher candidates to identify English Language Arts (ELA) writing lessons and/or English classes. Although these settings are, indeed, ripe with opportunities for students to practice and develop their writing skills, these skills are just as important for communication in other content areas.

Likewise, students of all ages engage in writing practices in a large array of contexts beyond the confines of a classroom. During a brainstorming session on the first day of our class, *The Art of Writing for Educators*, we often ask our teacher candidates to identify the types of writing present in their day-to-day lives. The outcomes of these conversations capture the many forms of writing, including the following: poems, song lyrics, shopping lists, resumes, restaurant order tickets, diaries, class notes, speeches, schedules, accident reports, texts, emails, social media posts, blogs, letters, thank you notes, and short stories. Although the teacher candidates frequently indicate that they had not previously stopped to think about the role of writing in their daily lives, the lists that they generate reflect the pervasiveness and varied nature of writing in which they naturally engage every day. Therefore, it is important to consider how teachers and teacher candidates at all grade levels can draw upon these everyday writing experiences in order to support their own students' learning about writing in varied forms. Perhaps students in a social studies class are asked to compose fictitious social media posts from the perspective of an historical figure. These types of activities provide students with opportunities to merge academic content with forms of communication with which they might be more comfortable or familiar.

However, as Wiggins and McTighe (2006) have pointed out in their description of the *backward design* approach to lesson and curriculum development, teachers must be mindful of how and for what purpose they design learning activities. These authors emphasized the importance of identifying lesson goals and assessment criteria *prior* to designing teaching and learning activities. "Though considerations about what to teach and how to teach it may dominate our thinking as a matter of habit, the challenge is to focus first on the desired learnings from which appropriate teaching will logically follow" (p. 14), as this supports the alignment of learning activities with lesson goals more effectively. The authors went on to state the following:

> The error of activity-oriented design might be called "hands-on without being minds-on"-engaging experiences that lead only accidentally, if at all, to insight or achievement. The activities, though fun and interesting, do not lead anywhere intellectually…such activity-oriented curricula lack an explicit focus on important ideas and appropriate evidence of learning, especially in the minds of learners. They think their job is merely to engage; they are led to think the learning *is* the activity instead of seeing that the learning comes from being asked to consider the *meaning* of the activity. (p. 16)

Therefore, when designing learning experiences that draw upon students' everyday writing experiences, teachers and teacher candidates should think carefully about how such activities support meaning making and align with the lesson's learning goals and objectives. In the example previously suggested, in which students in a social studies class write social media posts from the perspective of an historical figure, the teacher would need to specify the goal of creating such communications. For instance, a learning objective stating that *students will be able to write from the perspective of an historical figure* might not make visible the importance of communicating through seemingly informal modes of writing (i.e., social media posts). In contrast, an objective stating that *students will be able to compose texts conveying an historical figure's feelings about world events to invoke action in modern society* establishes the purpose of writing about an historical figure with the intent of encouraging reflection upon connections between historical and modern societies. The latter objective and the writing activity are more explicitly tied together not only to engage students in an enjoyable and relatable lesson activity, but also to support the students in considering lesson content through writing.

> ### Curriculum Matters: Connecting Writing within and beyond the Classroom
>
> As previously noted, students engage in multiple forms of writing in their everyday lives, and it is important for teachers to consider how to capitalize upon these daily experiences to support student learning.
>
> Here we encourage you to write a learning objective relevant to your content area, then consider different forms of "everyday" writing in which students typically engage that could be utilized to address this objective. Consider how this form of writing might be effective for addressing your identified learning objective by noting (a) the learning objective; (b) related type(s) of "everyday" writing; and (c) the way "everyday" writing might support your learning objective.

WRITING BEYOND THE ABC'S

Although writing is traditionally thought of in terms of alphabetic text, literacy research suggests that writing need not be bounded by letters on a page. In 1996, a group of researchers known as the New London Group published their foundational work, *A Pedagogy of Multiliteracies: Designing Social Futures,* to address a growing awareness of the multiple forms that communication might take, and they made a claim for an educational future that prepares—not suppresses—students for work, for life, and for societal contributions. The authors began by noting that "literacy pedagogy has traditionally meant teaching and learning to read and write in page-bound, official, standard forms of the national language" (p. 60), and then proposed a more comprehensive framework for multiliteracies in order to do the following:

> [T]o extend the idea and scope of literacy pedagogy to account for the context of our culturally and linguistically diverse and increasingly

> globalized societies…[and] argue that literacy pedagogy now must account for the burgeoning variety of text forms associated with information and multimedia technologies. (p. 61)

What the New London Group initiated—a reflection on pedagogy and practice and a call to action—has since explicitly and implicitly driven teacher education. Especially given the rapid pace of technological change, it is important to recognize and respond to multiple forms of texts and meaning making. For example, Cope et al. (2017) noted that, "readable matter is also found on phones and tablets and in e-books…we 'read' in videogames, apps, searchable web sources, and data mashups created on the fly. Written text is integrally juxtaposed with image, video, data visualization, and sound" (p. 38). What is key here is not the actual platform per se—be it a mobile phone or a videogame platform or an e-reader—but the meaning making that occurs with and through the text at hand.

Gunther Kress (2010) explained that "texts are always multimodal," which might seem odd at first, but makes perfect sense when you take into account that modes (e.g., sound, texture, image, movement, light, gesture) come together to produce meaning (p. 157). Take a moment to think about anything you have done—even something as mundane as washing the dishes. You are interacting with different modes, including the sensation of the water on your skin (or glove), the temperature of the water, the slipperiness of the soap, the degree of lighting that impacts the ways in which you perceive the sullied dishes, and so on. As you wash the dishes, you are making meaning. You are considering (a) what needs to be cleaned, (b) the extent to which it needs to be cleaned (is it a quick rinse? does the pan need to soak? do you need to scrub the dish?), and (c) what you consider clean to be. Although meaning making can and should involve greater critical thinking, we should not dismiss the ways in which multimodalities figure into everyday thinking and learning.

Once you have reached this point, you can start to think about and apply this expansive understanding of meaning making beyond print text (or the ABC's as we call it). You can also think about how it exists in everything we do, how it impacts your understanding of writing, and how it works towards current and future expressions of meaning. David Barton (2006) nodded to this exploration of other sign systems when he accounted for numeric, graphical, and non-alphabetic representations of meaning:

> [I]t is clear that in literacy events people use written language in an integrated way as part of a range of symbolic resources and

communicative resources; these resources include mathematical systems, graphics, maps and other non-text based images. The cookery text has numeracy mixed with print literacy and the recipes come from books, magazines, the internet, television, as well as orally from friends and relatives. (p. 24)

We contend that, especially given the affordances of digital resources, the layering of digital and nondigital experiences (Abrams, 2015, 2017), and the embodied representations of meaning (Burnett et al., 2014), there are opportunities to explore and expand meaning making through a continued revision and perhaps eradication of boundaries of what it means to make meaning. In this chapter, we focus on the digital story as one way to push against traditional silos that keep writing in English class and create opportunities to support *freedom* in writing, as well as writing for social change. After all, if your students and you can re-envision writing and the many forms it takes, then you all can create renewed forms of expression.

Viewing writing as a *cross-literate practice* (Abrams & Gerber, 2014) enables teachers of any discipline to build upon the ethos of *literacies*, which does not see literacy being solely about alphabetic text, but, rather, as meaning making that is the sum of our experiences (Street, 1999). Thus, when we talk about literate practices, we are focusing on ways students understand what they see (be it a beaker of solution or a resistance poem) and how they call upon their own experiences to interpret the material. What is more, we think about cross-literate practices and connections wherein students not only fold in their own experiences, but also take into account peer feedback while negotiating the "interweaving of modalities and disciplines" (Abrams & Gerber, 2014, p. 21).

We witnessed teacher candidates establishing cross-literate connections when designing and constructing digital stories that showcased expansive understandings of writing (Morabito & Abrams, 2015). For example, juxtaposing hockey with writing, two teacher candidates found symmetry in the process of planning (prewriting), practice (rough draft writing), feedback (peer review), game play (revised, final draft), and post-game debriefs (reflection). In their written reflection upon their digital story, these students further underscored the relatable aspects of cross-literate practices, as they saw "a connection between essay writing in classrooms and sports playing on courts, fields, and rinks," and they contended:

If teachers are able to make the connection between the two processes and help students understand that connection, it is more than likely that students who play sports but struggle with writing will be able to understand the writing process much better and therefore will understand the importance of each part and how it helps them to write better. (Digital Storytelling Reflection, p. 1)

In other words, there are important pedagogical implications to the inclusion of cross-literate practices. To provide an example of cross-literate practices that might be visible in a classroom setting, we ask you to consider the ways in which students in a physics class draw upon their own individual and collective experiences in and beyond the classroom as they also engage with mathematical models. In such classes, students are asked to use mathematical representations to construct meaning of patterns in the natural world (e.g., Newton's second law of motion used to understand the relationships among force, mass, and acceleration). Through their cross-literate connections, students would go beyond simply using the equation (i.e., Force = mass x acceleration) to complete a calculation and, instead, consider the meaning of the representation and calculation *together* to construct understandings of the movement of objects in the world around us. For instance, students who have played the game, *Angry Birds,* might think about how "the slingshot and the different birds cause acceleration to change based on the stretch of the slingshot and the bird's size" (Arroyo, n.d.) in relation to underlying physics principles. Similarly, students studying Newton's second law might perform calculations and consider the relationships among the different parts of the equation used to understand the concept of motion when riding a bike. That is, as riders apply an increasing amount of *force* to the bike pedals using their legs, and given that the *mass* remains constant, the *acceleration* will, consequently, change over time.

Curriculum Matters: Media Literacy

The Featured Assignment addressed in this chapter draws upon another type of literacy not yet addressed, but important to acknowledge: *media* literacy. The National Association for Media Literacy Education (NAMLE) defines media literacy as follows:

Media literacy is the ability to ACCESS, ANALYZE, EVALUATE, CREATE, and ACT using all forms of communication. In its simplest terms, media literacy builds upon the foundation of traditional literacy and offers new forms of reading and writing. Media literacy empowers people to be critical thinkers and makers, effective communicators and active citizens. (Media Literacy Defined section, n.d., para. 1)

NAMLE then delineates this definition further to capture key aspects of this form of literacy:

- Media refers to all electronic or digital means and print or artistic visuals used to transmit messages
- Literacy is the ability to encode and decode symbols and to synthesize and analyze messages
- Media literacy is the ability to encode and decode the symbols transmitted via media and the ability to synthesize, analyze and produce mediated messages
- Media education is the study of media, including 'hands on' experiences and media production
- Media literacy education is the educational field dedicated to teaching the skills associated with media literacy (Media Literacy Defined section, n.d., para. 2)

Just as we, as educators, support the development of literacy in more traditional academic domains, we value the need to attend to media literacy, as well. The digital storytelling assignment described in this chapter is designed, in part, to support media literacy development by providing an opportunity for teachers and teacher candidates to explore teaching and learning through the composition of a media-based form of communication.

Many scholars have written about media literacy, including, but not limited to, Hobbs and Jensen (2009), Hobbs and Moore (2013), Koltay (2011), Livingstone and van der Graaf (2010), and Potter (2019). These suggested works will help readers interested in exploring this line of inquiry further.

DIGITAL STORYTELLING FOR EXAMINING TEACHING AND LEARNING SPACES

Think of a book that you have read that you have subsequently seen adapted into a movie. How were the stories in these two formats similar, and how did they differ? In some instances, aspects of the written text might have been omitted (e.g., certain characters), while other aspects might have been expanded upon. Certain story details might be altered in the film version in the interest of clarity, or entirely new material might be introduced that takes the story in a different direction. How did such additions and/or omissions impact the story being told? Did you feel as though one medium was more successful in conveying the intended story/message? Did the story arc remain the same, or did the story in the movie differ fundamentally from the book? If the latter, how did this impact the reader's/viewer's experience with the story being told?

In addition to pure story content, consider the visual and auditory affordances and constraints that arose when the book was adapted into a film. Were any portions of the story enhanced by being made into a film version, perhaps through the use of sounds, music, lighting, and/or visual effects to evoke certain moods or emotions? How did the characters that you envisioned in your mind while reading the book compare to their on-screen portrayals by the actors in the movie? Did the actors' portrayals bring the characters to life for you, or did you find their differences from your own mental imagery distracting? If material was omitted when adapting the book into a movie, how did the filmmakers attempt to fill in any gaps that were created in doing so? For instance, did they include voiceover narration and/ or flashbacks to address such gaps and ensure story continuity? If so, how might this impact the reader's/viewer's experience with the story being told?

We ask you to consider these similarities and differences not to engage in an in-depth media study, but to encourage you to start thinking about how messages might be conveyed through these two different formats. Previously in this chapter we discussed some of the different forms that writing can take, and here we begin to explore how messages can be conveyed through yet another medium: *digital storytelling*. Essentially, whether based on fiction or non-fiction, movies are intended to tell stories. Similarly, digital stories provide another medium through which teachers and students can convey and reflect upon their own understandings of a particular topic through short multimedia stories. As when books are adapted into movies, composing a digital story can provide ways for the storyteller to highlight a message using tools that are not available when composing, say, a typewritten essay. Therefore, digital storytelling provides a unique medium through which students (and teachers and teacher candidates) can communicate their understandings and thoughts on a vast array of topics. Before moving into a description of the Featured Assignment, we will discuss the roles that digital storytelling can play in building literacy skills, supporting content knowledge, promoting meaning making, and sustaining reflection.

Composing and Visualizing Text through Digital Media

Have you ever found yourself struggling to "get words on paper" in order to complete a conventional writing assignment, perhaps wishing that you could use another approach for conveying your ideas to an audience? Perhaps you're tired of doing the "same old thing" by writing yet another essay or term paper. It could be that you have difficulty finding the "right" words to adequately represent your thinking or feelings. If you have ever felt this way about composing a written piece of work, you might find the concept of composing a digital story to be compelling. Research has shown that engaging teachers in digital storytelling supports them in multiple ways, including developing a sense of community (Chigona, 2013), understanding the integral roles of technology in the classroom (e.g., Doering et al., 2007; Heo, 2009), and understanding multimodal literacy practices (Miller, 2007).

Digital storytelling provides opportunities for individuals to use images, music, and video clips to enhance (or completely stand in for) written text when communicating a message to an audience. As David Bruce (2008), stated, "In written composition, it may be that students who struggle with print have a difficult time conveying their thoughts using traditional conventions" (p. 266). For these reasons, digital storytelling is considered a useful platform for supporting students of all ages as they build and refine their literacy skills. It also provides a rich opportunity for addressing the needs of diverse learners, as students can use a variety of modalities to communicate their thinking. Through digital storytelling, individuals can explore how written text can be represented and interwoven with other forms of representation. In so doing, composers of digital stories engage in a range of multimodal literacy practices as they hone the messages for their intended audience(s).

In addition to literacy skills, digital storytelling provides opportunities for students, teacher candidates, and teachers to build content knowledge and promote meaning making in relation to this content. Jason Ohler (2013) pointed out that digital stories "allow today's students to pursue academic content in their own language" (p. 11). This might provide opportunities for students to find more personal relevance in and/or connection to academic content. For example, while exploring writing through digital storytelling in our class, many of our teacher candidates focused on writing in contexts with personal relevance. From exploring writing in science classrooms and work settings, to depicting the process of writing and revising song lyrics, to examining the meanings of text and images found in tattoos, to analyzing the role of sketching out potential plays during hockey practice, our teacher candidates identified the role of writing in settings to which they had personal connections (e.g., themselves, friends, and family). Thus, they were able to draw upon and convey their developing understandings of the roles of writing in a variety of school-based and non-academic contexts.

One final aspect of digital storytelling that we find particularly beneficial for our teacher candidates is the manner in which the composition of a digital story sustains reflection. (We discuss the role of reflective practices in greater depth in Chapter 4, but the importance of digital storytelling for reflection warrants attention here.) Although you will see that we ask you to reflect upon the digital storytelling experience as a concluding aspect of your exploration of cross-literate practices, the composition process, itself, helps support reflection and foster reflective teaching practice. In prior work (Morabito & Abrams, 2015), we provided examples of how the digital storytelling assignment supported our teacher candidates in reflecting upon the role of writing within and beyond the classroom. For instance, one of our teacher candidates wrote the following in her Digital Storytelling Reflection: "Part of the learning process is reflecting on one's work. I think that the digital story creation process involved reflection at every stage," and we noted that this student's "perception of reflection included an expansive understanding of metacognition in relation to overall learning" (Morabito & Abrams, 2015, p. 73). Therefore, reflection upon one's understanding of writing is an inherent part of the digital storytelling assignment.

With respect to teacher and teacher candidate development, we view the digital storytelling assignment to be valuable not only as a model for a teaching strategy that you can employ with your students, but also as a means for supporting your own understanding of the role of writing in education: "Overall, the recursive learning experiences [of composing a digital story] that emphasized multimodal production provided diverse means for the students to explore teaching and learning within and beyond the classroom" (Morabito & Abrams, 2015, p. 75). For this reason, we hope that the assignment described in the following section will challenge you to reconsider your own thinking about writing in relation to your current or future teaching and support you should you choose to engage your own students in digital storytelling.

Curriculum Matters: Telling a Story Through Images/Video

You have probably heard the expression "a picture is worth a thousand words." In the digital storytelling assignment described in this chapter, we invite you to consider creating a sequence of images and/or video, along with accompanying narration, to tell a story about teaching and learning.

Before you move forward with this assignment, consider the story told about Integrated Studies at the following link: https://www.edutopia.org/video/introduction-integrated-studies. Watch the video and jot down your thoughts in response to the following questions: (a) what is the story the narrator is telling; (b) how does the narrator use specific video clips to support the argument; (c) when does the narrator speak, and (d) what is the purpose of this narration or absence of it?

One dimension of digital storytelling we must remain aware of is the fact that no digital story is a neutral text, underscoring a point made in previous chapters. The perceptions, perspectives, and, potentially, biases of the creator(s) of a digital story all come to bear on its contents. Have you ever watched a documentary and wondered whether the message presented is fully representative of the issue addressed? Does it appear to be rather one-sided with respect to the issue at hand? If so, this might be because the creators made production and editorial decisions to focus on specific information in support of their own argument. Consider the aforementioned *Integrated Studies* video. While the creators certainly make a convincing argument for the importance and effectiveness of this particular curricular approach, might they have intentionally left out information about other, potentially contradictory, approaches to teaching and learning that also have been shown to have been beneficial for students? If so, why might they have done so? How might this impact the message conveyed to you, as the viewer? While composing a digital story, the creators must make similar decisions regarding what content to use to support their argument. Additionally, creators must consider and acknowledge whose stories are being told, whose voices are being represented, and what omissions or silenced voices remain. Therefore, the creators' (or creator's) beliefs about and understandings of the topic addressed have an inherent influence on the message conveyed.

FEATURED ASSIGNMENT: CREATING A DIGITAL STORY TO
EXPLORE WRITING ACROSS CONTEXTS

Having discussed the powerful nature of digital storytelling, we now move into a description of the assignment focused on composing digital stories about writing. This assignment asks you, as a teacher or teacher candidate, to work with a partner to present your understanding of teaching and learning spaces for writing in a variety of contexts and environments through a short digital story. Therefore, you will need to select a topic related to writing, create a storyboard outlining the content you will want to address in each segment of your digital story, generate a script for any voiceover narration that you might include in the digital story, record video of people engaging in the type(s) of writing you choose to address, and, finally, compile and edit your video into one cohesive, yet succinct, digital story depicting and explaining what writing topic you chose to explore. After you have completed the digital story, your partner and you will write a reflective narrative about the affordances and limitations of video recorded "stories." In what follows, we describe in greater detail these steps toward completion of the digital storytelling assignment.

First, though, as educators, we are all too familiar with the age-old student question, "Why do we have to do this?" You might be wondering the same in relation to the digital storytelling assignment. How might this help you as a current or future teacher? When we originally designed this assignment, we intended it to support our teacher candidates in not only thinking about the pervasive nature of writing within and across content areas, but also helping engage them with the writing process in ways with which they might not have had much experience (e.g., composing a storyboard and script, telling a story using video and images). What we have found is that the creation of the digital story has engaged our teacher candidates in thinking deeply about their ideas about teaching, as well as their own writing. As you will see in a sample of student work contained later in this chapter, one pair of teacher candidates in our class reflected upon the assignment by noting that, "Since empathy and engagement are the keys to becoming active learners… providing…future students with an outlet to connect with the material in a way that is directly relatable to them would in turn…enhance their educational experience." Another pair of teacher candidates reflected upon implications of the assignment for their future completion of the edTPA. Given that the video portion of this assessment task is, in some ways, a form of digital storytelling highlighting an individual's approach to teaching, they stated the following:

> This assignment showed us that with persistence and patience we can find an effective way to get our message across when time is a limiting factor. This is a critical thing to keep in mind for the video portion of the edTPA, as we will have to find a way to maximize instructional minutes to best display our teaching abilities.

Furthermore, the range of topics selected by teacher candidates has been far more expansive than we ever anticipated. Through their explorations of writing in traditional school-based settings, as well as many forms of writing that take place outside school (e.g., writing in professional office settings, composing music for a band, exploring tattoos as a medium for personal expression, drawing plays to be used in a hockey game), our teacher candidates have come to appreciate the importance of writing throughout all aspects of their lives. Therefore, we see the creation of a digital story as an important exercise in thinking about one's own understanding of writing, as well as the implications of this understanding for one's teaching.

The following sections provide you with more details regarding the process of creating your digital story, starting with brainstorming ideas for a topic and concluding with the composition of a written reflection on the digital storytelling process. We intentionally have broken down the process into phases in order to make the project more manageable, as well as to provide built-in checkpoints for those who might be using this text in a teacher education course.

Creating Your Digital Story Phase A: Topic Selection

With your partner, you will need to select one aspect of the writing/thinking process that you would like to examine. Be sure to consider the following:

1. Would I/we prefer to focus on writing in a school-based learning environment and, if so, in what type of setting (e.g., a particular content area or grade level)?
2. If interested in writing outside the classroom, is there some form of writing/thinking that I/we find personally important that I/we would like to explore through digital storytelling?

Please note that, once you begin videotaping, you might notice something else you would like to explore or discuss. Therefore, we encourage you to remain open to changing your topic once your recording is underway. Such a shift in topic/focus will need to be part of the reflective narrative that you will write at the end of the digital storytelling assignment in order to explain to the reader how and why your thinking and focus might have changed.

Next, you will need to determine what learning experiences your partner and you will focus on and videotape (e.g., writing workshops, process writing, journal writing, online writing, writing in content areas other than ELA). We suggest that your focal learning experiences occur in at least two different learning environments. These learning environments might represent any combination of formal and/or informal settings, so do not feel confined only to the classroom.

You might notice that this step is related to one of the strategies discussed at length in Chapter 2 (i.e., gather multiple sources of evidence). Indeed, in this assignment you are asked to collect evidence in the form of video to support your claim about the writing that you have chosen to examine. We ask you to focus on recording learning in at least two different environments in order to accrue at least two distinct, rich sources of evidence. You likely will draw upon other evidence (e.g., academic texts), which can be incorporated into the script that you will develop in a future step of this assignment, to further bolster your claims.

Creating Your Digital Story Phase B: Storyboarding and Script Development

In order to help you plan your Digital Story, you should create a storyboard describing what you intend to examine in your video. The creation of your storyboard will help you begin to organize your thinking about what types of video footage you might want to record and in what order you want to present your ideas. Storyboard templates are widely available online via a Google search. They serve as graphic organizers for brainstorming and arranging images, along with any respective captions and narration. Sample templates[1] can be found at sites such as:

- https://habitualfilms.files.wordpress.com/2011/05/storyboard-template-2.jpg
- https://www.utdallas.edu/atec/midori/Handouts/storyboard_files/template2.jpg

You should use the boxes to sketch *what* you plan to video. Then use the accompanying lines to jot down notes regarding *who* will be speaking, *scene transitions*, and any other *sound* that you might use (e.g., music). As you create your storyboard, you might need to leave some boxes blank until you begin video recording and fill them in once you know what footage you are able to record. Please be aware that, although this video will be for a class assignment and should not be distributed publicly, filming in schools likely will require you to get permission of families, the teacher, and/or the school.

A sample storyboard created by two of our teacher candidates can be found in Figure 1. As you review the sample, consider the following:

- What types of information is included for each scene that the authors have planned?
- What story is being told through the scenes? How is it introduced and developed?
- How might this information help the authors as they begin the recording process?

Once you have developed a draft of your storyboard, you should begin to outline a narration script for your video; this script is separate from, but is related to, your storyboard. It can include (but is not limited to) voice-over narration, on-screen captions, and/or character lines (if you integrate yourself into the video). Keep in mind that your script can evolve as you film your video.

After completing draft versions of your storyboard and script, we highly recommend that you utilize yet another practice described in Chapter 2— engaging in a writing workshop. This will provide your partner and you an opportunity to solicit feedback from peers about the contents and flow of your storyboard and script, and to discuss your plans for video recording before beginning the actual recording process.

The following example features an excerpt from a script developed by two of our teacher candidates. Although this sample does not correspond with the storyboard in Figure 1, it should help you get a sense of the types of information included in this portion of the assignment. As you read the sample, consider the following:

- What types of information is conveyed through the text that would eventually be included as voiceover narration?
- How do the authors set the stage for each of the scenes to be accompanied by their narration? That is, what information do they include aside from the words that would be recorded as voiceover narration?
- What other information might have been helpful to include?
- How are the types of information included in a script similar to and/or different from the types of information included in a storyboard?

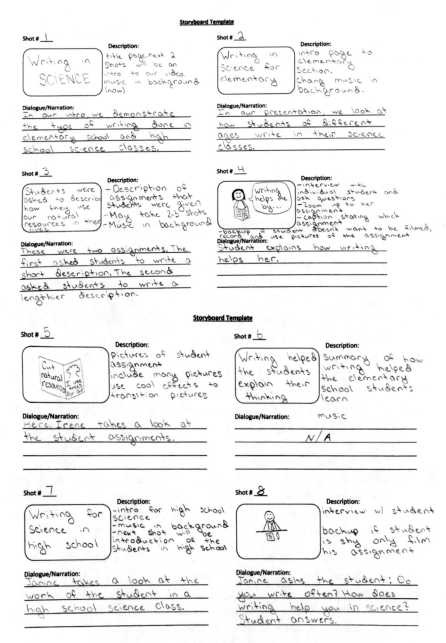

Figure 1. An excerpt from a sample storyboard

Example of Student Work: Excerpt from a Digital Story Script

Scene 1

Here we will have quotes saying that there is a writing crisis. The quotes will be accompanied by sad music and will be narrated.

Samantha:	"Writing in Schools is found both dismal and neglected" (Lewin, 2003).
Alicia:	"American students today are not meeting even basic writing standards" (Graham & Perin, 2007, p. 2).

Scene 2

Here we will have a summary of how we plan on showing that we are no longer in a writing crisis. It will be narrated but instead will be accompanied by happy music.

Samantha:	Today we will look at how writing is occurring more than ever before.
Alicia:	We will explore this topic in two different environments: the workplace and the home.
Pamela:	Let's have a look at the workplace where we will see how and when writing occurs throughout the day.

Scene 3

A clip of work being done in an office will be shown. We will freeze frame on times when we want to show how the people are writing. We will address this through voice overs.

Alicia:	Here we see Catherine, Morgan, Linda and Molly working in the office.
Samantha:	It might seem that there isn't a lot of writing but let's take a closer look.

Freeze frame

Alicia:	When we look closer we can see that there are actually multiple types of writing occurring.
Samantha:	Catherine is typing on the computer, Molly is writing in her notebook, Linda is texting on her phone and Morgan is practicing sign language.

Alicia:	These might not all be traditional, but they are all forms of writing. With new types of technology it seems like people are writing more than ever before.

Creating Your Digital Story Phase C: Recording Your Video Footage

Now that you have outlined your digital story using your storyboard and developed a script for your narration, it is time to begin filming. Using a recording device of your choice (e.g., digital video recorder, tablet, phone), capture video of people engaging in the forms of writing upon which you have chosen to focus. How can you (quite literally) *show*, not *tell*, your viewer your story through the video footage that you collect?

You might wish to simultaneously take some still photos of these moments of writing for use during the following phase of your digital story development. Also, be prepared to take multiple videos, as your initial recording might not go as you had planned. For example, there might be problems with sound, or you might find that you lack adequate storage space on your recording device. Although recording videos is a common pastime, this type of recording often requires more time for planning, filming, editing, and revising.

Creating Your Digital Story Phase D: Editing & Revising

Once you have collected your video footage, it is time to begin the editing process using video editing software such as iMovie or Windows Movie Maker. You should think carefully about how to trim and splice together your video segments in order to make the most compelling argument about writing in your selected context(s). What parts can be reduced or eliminated? How might you splice together your video clips to show (again, not just tell) the most coherent story about the aspect of writing on which you have focused? What visual effects might be used to smooth transitions between scenes?

You should revisit your narration script to revise and refine it based on the contents of your video, and then add voice and/or print narration to the video itself as needed. This narration should guide your audience to understand not only what you're seeing, but also *what is not seen* and how the unseen is part of your story. For example, the video made by one pair of our teacher candidates focused on a peer who was composing a song for his band. Given the length of time required to engage in this writing process, the teacher candidates chose to show clips of the musician composing at an accelerated pace, as if "fast forwarding" through the video footage. While this acceleration concealed the actual amount of time required for this writing process, it essentially allowed the viewer to see it in its entirety.

You also should consider what other audio adjustments or effects might be needed. Would music enhance any portions of your story? If so, what style would be most effective at enhancing without distracting the viewer? If it is difficult to hear any of the spoken audio captured, might on-screen captions be needed?

As you prepare to move on to the final step of this assignment and submit your completed digital story, this is an optimal time for engaging in another writing workshop. In this workshop, your partner and you can share your video, along with the accompanying storyboard and script, to obtain peer feedback on all three components of the assignment that you have completed to date. For instance, how well does the digital story convey your message about and understandings of writing in your chosen settings? Do the final storyboard and script accurately outline what is depicted in the digital story itself? If not, what adjustments are needed?

Creating Your Digital Story Phase E: Reflecting on the Digital Storytelling Experience

As previously noted, after completing your Digital Story, you are asked to write a reflective narrative (either individually or collaboratively with your partner) about the creation and content of your digital story. This reflective narrative should address what is highlighted and also what is not seen because of the camera's positioning—in essence, you will need to "fill in the gaps" to explore the affordances and limitations communicating via digital storytelling.

Also, your reflection is a place for you to consider what video material your partner and you have chosen to privilege in your digital story. As noted previously, no text, whether written or in the form of a digital story, is neutral. Therefore, you are asked to consider the perspectives and potential biases that have come to bear on your decision-making during the creation of your digital story. That is, why did you choose to represent writing in the way that you did? Perhaps more importantly, what did you choose not to show and/or address in some way? For instance, in the interest of time and/ or for privacy concerns you might have chosen to omit footage of a child struggling with a particular writing task. How might that omission impact the story that was told? What might have been missed with respect to how struggling writers approach (or are discouraged from approaching) certain forms of writing based on your editing decisions? It is important to consider not only what your partner and you chose to include, but also what you chose not to incorporate into your digital story.

To conclude your reflection, you should discuss the potential use of digital storytelling in your own current or future teaching. How might you use digital storytelling to help your own students in developing their understandings of writing? What benefits and/or drawbacks might you see with respect to the use of digital storytelling in your own classroom?

We have included sample reflections composed by some of our teacher candidates. As you read the samples, consider the following:

- How do the authors explain their reasoning for focusing on their selected topics related to writing?
- How do the authors address what is not visible in their digital stories?
- What benefits and/or drawbacks do the authors identify with respect to using digital storytelling in their own teaching?

Example of Student Work: Excerpt from Digital Storytelling Reflection A

If the key to higher learning is engagement, then digital storytelling helps to unlock the door. As preservice teachers like myself prepare to take on classes filled with digital natives for students, reflection is an essential part of one's own interaction with digital tools that may someday be used in one's classroom.

The primary focus of the narrative produced by Carrie and I is how routine writing assignments geared toward maximizing student input can enhance content learning. Because we both firmly support student-centered activities, Carrie and I felt that highlighting *why* journaling is an asset to adolescent education was of utmost importance throughout this project. To emphasize this, we incorporated two interviews in which we asked a middle and a high school student to elaborate on how routine writing assignments help them to expand on content learning. Each of us then provided several recaps to elaborate on what future teachers should take away from the students' testimony. We felt that the assets of journaling were best expressed by students who participate in journaling on an everyday basis because their statements as well as the enthusiasm they convey are direct evidence of how journaling can be utilized to engage students in any area and at either end of the adolescent spectrum.

Although our video did provide an in-depth analysis of adolescent journaling, Carrie and I had to go to great lengths to elaborate on what we could not directly show on film. Perhaps the most obvious example is how neither of our interview subjects could be filmed while writing in the classroom for legal reasons. Because viewers could not see journaling being implemented, Carrie and I provided examples of the subjects' writing artifacts as well as teaching recaps to explain how journaling *does* and *should* manifest in the classroom. By using animated recap slides as well as captions and narration to clearly separate the students' perspective from the implications of their statements for preservice teachers seeking to utilize journaling as a classroom tool, Carrie and I adequately compensated for the lack of "live-action" journaling footage to draw from.

As a whole, our experience with digital storytelling proved to be a mixed one. One issue that Carrie and I frequently ran into throughout the editing and publishing processes, for instance, was technical difficulties. Because neither Carrie and I have extensive experience using digital media, we often found ourselves lost as to how to correct errors such as audio-video being out of sync. As a teacher, I would be sure to invite a media expert such as a computer skills teacher into the classroom to help my students erect technical errors throughout the editing process. Overall, I truly believe that digital storytelling offers extensive benefits for both students and teachers. In this project I loved how I was able to connect with students on a very honest level. Because I was speaking with them in their homes instead of in the classroom, I felt that they were much more comfortable with providing me with their "gut" feelings toward journaling; this in turn allowed both Carrie and I to provide our viewers with valuable teaching advice that will actually *work*. As a preservice English teacher, I would definitely be inclined to use digital storytelling as a creative outlet for my students to, for instance, re-enact a scene from a play or present film versions of personal narratives they've written. Since empathy and engagement are the keys to becoming active learners in an English/Language Arts setting, providing my future students with an outlet to connect with the material in a way that is directly relatable to them would in turn allow me as teacher to enhance their educational experience.

Example of Student Work: Excerpt from Digital Storytelling Reflection B

What is highlighted and why is that information important?
One thing that was highlighted in our video that we wanted to emphasize was the process that goes into creating a sketch or a web page. Often, we view art and websites without keeping in mind the process that goes into making them. There is an idea, a composition process, and an end result that communicates a message. We wanted to illustrate that process and show it as a form of writing and communication. Our overall message to the viewers was that there are multiple forms of composition and that they should not be afraid of thinking outside of the box.

What is not shown and how effective are the techniques used to "fill the gaps?" Explain. What are the affordances and limitations of digital stories?
Our introduction sound was that of a typewriter because we felt that it was simple and would capture the viewers' attention. We used still images to advance our digital story and to support the narration. When we were not narrating, the subjects in our video were answering questions highlighted by on screen captions. We chose not to narrate or use audio while our subjects were speaking because we felt it would take away from the natural aspect of the video. Another reason that we chose to substitute narration for captions was because it would have taken more time to record and edit the narration to fit each frame. While John was drawing we could hear his pencil making lines and his eraser when he made a change. These sound effects were real and sufficient for the drawing portion. There were points in the video where we both wanted to add more audio, but decided against it because we wanted to be mindful of how the final product would sound. It was essential for us to make sure that the audio was not distorted or overlapping in a way that would hinder the audience from hearing what was most important. We made sure to add smooth transitions between frames so it would maintain a consistent flow. Using the stills helped to emphasize our idea and illustrate the link between our two subtopics.

For our first interview, John did not want to be on camera. This presented a small challenge because the purpose of filming him was to show how passionate he is when drawing. Filming just his hand had a very different effect than being able to see the artist as he composes. In order to compensate for that, we filmed from over John's shoulder showing only his profile. Filming from the side as opposed to straight on created another problem, as John's interview answers were harder to hear. Some things were hidden in the video due to our time constraint, such as Steven typing the extended coding that produced his webpage as well as John's entire process of sketching. To compensate for these hidden aspects, we highlighted a glimpse of the beginning, middle, and end of each process as opposed to its entirety.

Another challenge was filming with low quality cameras and equipment. Today we do most of our filming with our smartphones, but they are not high-end equipment. We expected to be able to modify the volume using the tools on WeVideo, but that was not a feature on the website. We are also perfectionists and this caused some problems because no matter how much we edited, we kept finding faults. This is something that we will definitely consider in the future because we will most likely have students who will be their own worst critic. Despite our perfectionist ideals, our limitations were centered around technical issues such as audio and visual.

As future teachers, we will have to account for the supplies and time our students will have to complete this assignment. We both hope to teach very young children (Aria wants to teach second grade and Maya wants to teach fourth) and agree that a digital storytelling assignment would be too much to expect of children at these ages. We agree that digital storytelling could be an effective teaching tool at this general grade level as a way to summarize a unit or project and to showcase student work and progress to parents. In this way we can give students a sense of ownership and pride in their work as they see it displayed in this dynamic format. This assignment showed us that with persistence and patience we can find an effective way to get our message across when time is a limiting factor. This is a critical thing to keep in mind for the video portion of the edTPA, as we will have to find a way to maximize instructional minutes to best display our teaching abilities.

CONCLUDING THOUGHTS: WRITING TOWARD THE FUTURE

This chapter focused on writing in a variety of contexts and forms, with the goal of supporting teachers and teacher candidates as they engage their own (future and current) students in different forms of composition. We began by highlighting the enduring presence of writing in students' everyday lives, as well as the means by which students might engage in writing across educational contexts. This then led into discussions of multiliteracies and the forms that writing might take beyond traditional alphabetic text. In order to tie all of these elements together, you explored your own understandings of writing though the development of and reflection upon a digital story related to writing.

Through this sequence of reading, thinking, and activity, we aim to expand upon traditional notions of writing and challenge you to consider not only your own understandings of writing, but also the possibilities for your own students' writing within and beyond the classroom. We encourage you to be mindful of the ever-expanding landscape of platforms for writing and composition in your own students' lives and consider how you can draw upon them to engage students in meaningful writing activities.

Questions for Further Consideration

1. In thinking about your own teaching, what opportunities might there be for you to engage *your students* in digital storytelling? What issues of equity and access exist? What resources might you need in order to support your students in digital storytelling (e.g., technology teachers, computers, digital recording equipment)?
2. How might digital storytelling help address the needs of the diverse learners in your own current or future classroom?
3. How might digital storytelling address and/or complicate issues of power and privilege in writing instruction?

NOTE

1   The links provided in this chapter are live as of the time of publication. In the event that the links to these materials are no longer functioning or additional resources are needed, an online search for the term "storyboard" should yield multiple results.

REFLECTING ON REFLECTIVE PRACTICES

GUIDING QUESTIONS

This chapter invites you to explore reflective practices in and around writing. As you read this chapter, please consider the following guiding questions:

1. What are your assumptions about teaching? How do you purposefully or inadvertently fold those assumptions into your current and/or future practice? What judgements do you make?
2. How does context impact the way you discuss teaching practices? Think about how you document the classroom space and how, if at all, you acknowledge student learning in light of social, cultural, historical, economical, and political factors that could be shaping students' work, teacher's practices, and your interpretations of the students' work and teacher's practices?

INTRODUCTION

Reflective practice has long been an important part of teaching. In *The Reflective Practitioner*, Donald Schön (1983) emphasized the need for educators to reflect in two capacities: as they teach, or *reflection-in-action*, as well as after class ends, or *reflection-on-action*. Although reflection typically occurs after an action takes place, Schön's work highlights the importance of reflection in-the-moment. This also is known as reflexive practice because there is continuous engagement in the process of learning. As such, Schön called attention to the ongoing, iterative nature of reflective thinking that is, at its core, part of a larger meaning making process. After all, it is through reflection-in-action that teachers, who are responsive to students' needs, can pivot their practice to accommodate individual learners or groups of students.

When addressing reflective and reflexive writing, Gillie Bolton (2010) explained that both "are essential for responsible and ethical practice" and both enable people to be accountable for their words and their actions (p. 5). Similar to Bolton's *through-the-mirror* writing, which involves a deep introspection to help educators discover how their beliefs and values inform

© ELIZABETH CHASE, NANCY P. MORABITO AND SANDRA SCHAMROTH ABRAMS, 2020 | DOI: 10.1163/9789004437265_004

practice, we suggest that teachers and teacher candidates consider the context and situated nature of their practice. This means thinking not only about their past experiences, but also their current ones: who they are in the moment, who their students are, and what the scenario is at that very moment in the classroom.

In this chapter, we focus on reflective and reflexive practices with regard to teacher candidates' writing in, about, and beyond teaching and learning. The Featured Assignment, the portfolio, presents a multidimensional approach to reflecting on reflective practices. Furthermore, because we embed our discussion in Schön's work, we use the term, *reflection*, throughout this chapter. However, because Schön talks about reflection-in-action and reflection-on-action, reflexivity is part of the conversation. We take this one step further to address writing that teachers and teacher candidates engage in professionally.

REFLECTION-IN-WRITING/REFLECTION-ON-WRITING

Just as Schön addressed reflection-in-action and reflection-on-action, we contend that there needs to be reflection-in-writing wherein teachers and teacher candidates reflect in the moment they are writing, as well as reflection-on-writing, which involves peer- and self-review of written work and opportunities to revise (vis-à-vis the writing process noted in Chapter 2). Reflection-in-writing might seem to be solitary in nature because one is reflecting while engaging in one's own writing. However, it is anything but solitary. After all, reflecting upon what is written, why it is written, and how one feels while composing involves thinking beyond oneself to account for context. Background and foreground experiences are essential to address. For instance, a teacher penning feedback for a student will need to consider (a) what is written (e.g., the words selected, their connotations and denotations, and how they might be interpreted), (b) why the feedback is written (e.g., what is the purpose of the particular feedback), and (c) how the teacher feels writing it (e.g., is the teacher excited? disappointed? annoyed? exhausted?). What is more, the teacher needs to consider other factors, including, but not limited to, how the student has been performing, what circumstances might be affecting student performance, and how the teacher's own experiences might color such interpretations. Emotions can and often will seep metaphorically through the ink and onto the student's paper, which potentially can be motivating or damaging. Reflecting-in-writing and reflecting-on-writing will inform the caliber, form, and tone of the teacher's feedback and overall communication.

Reflection-in-writing and reflection-on-writing, however, also can help students and teachers alike pay greater attention to the features and quality of their work. For instance, think about how you might begin writing *anything*—a letter, a list, an essay—and what happens when you realize you need to change something. You might cross out a word, sneak in a missing letter, or write an amendment on the side. Regardless, you are doing this in the moment. Such reflection-in-writing is different from completing a writing activity and returning to it at a later date. Through reflection-on-writing, you have the privilege of time and space to contemplate the writing with a level of unfamiliarity and distance, or *distal unfamiliarity*; distal unfamiliarity essentially means that there has been enough space between the time you have written your work (be it a list or an essay) and when you return to it so that you can question, "What did I mean when I said this?" instead of filling in the gaps with assumed and intended meaning.

We contend that teachers and teacher candidates must engage in reflection-in-writing *and* reflection-on-writing if they are going to think critically, honestly, and authentically about their instructional practices. This also dovetails well with a strategy that you read about in Chapter 2—engaging in peer review. In what follows, we unpack these concepts as we address field notes and other forms of reflective writing in which teachers and teacher candidates not only consider what they see and what they do, but also account for the experiences that might generate biases and myopic thinking. Thus, this chapter offers practical approaches to refining, enhancing, and revitalizing teachers' and teacher candidates' lifelong writing and learning.

Curriculum Matters: Reflecting Is Not Venting

Although reflecting upon one's day or a particular event might include a retelling of events and a sprinkling (or, at times, an inundation) of emotional responses, the type of reflection we discuss here is not a form of venting. Merriam-Webster defines "vent" as "to give often vigorous or emotional expression to" and "to relieve by means of a vent" ("Vent," n.d.). Both of these definitions include intense action. It might be possible that, as you observe a class or a social interaction among students, you recall a particular situation that occurred in your past. Or it might be possible that a student or teacher says or does something offensive. Whereas it is appropriate to record the event *and* your reactions to it, your notetaking should not include a cathartic rant or vent.

Likewise, it is imperative that any and all observations you conduct remain on paper and *not* find their way onto social media or other public outlets. We three have seen instances of teachers posting about something a student has done or something that occurred in their classroom. Even if no student names are used, such a post is a violation of student privacy, a breach of trust, and an unprofessional tack. We recognize that teachers and teacher candidates alike will have good and bad days. Keep those moments off social media and out of the public eye.

Effective reflection-in-writing and reflection-on-writing will help you to craft professional noticings that will help support your ever-evolving educational practice. In the event that you are having an off day, such a stance will help you catch yourself in the act of composing something that could be damaging to a child's self-esteem, to your school's reputation, or to your professional integrity.

FIELD NOTES AND REFLECTIVE WRITING IN EDUCATION

The practice of reflective teaching and writing is not completed only by teachers and in solitude. Rather, as we contend, reflective teaching and writing is an essential part of teacher candidate education, and it involves recording and sharing information about what one has seen, heard, and perceived in a classroom. Each time a teacher candidate steps foot into a formal (or informal) learning space, that educator-in-training is learning via observation and any hands-on opportunities to teach. Likewise, current teachers might experience such learning opportunities while observing in other classrooms in their own school, in another school in their district, or even in schools in other parts of the world.

Field notes (written notations while observing another's teaching) and reflective memos (informal post-observation debriefs) are records that might capture a moment in time, but they are living, social documents because they become part of the larger discussion of teaching and learning; teachers and teacher candidates look to field notes and memos to deconstruct practice, to consider applications of theory, to contemplate what they would replicate and change, and to engage in active reflection *with* colleagues or classmates to determine and refine their pedagogical stances and understandings of educational practices. Yet writing field notes and reflective memos is not an easy task, and simply assigning teachers or teacher candidates observational tasks will not support them in their journey.

Almost without fail, each semester, teacher candidates ask us about *how* to take field notes. Our immediate response is to engage in a conversation about (a) what an observation entails, (b) what types of questions to consider, and (c) how to document the role of the observer. Although we also provide examples of field notes, we have found it most helpful to call upon qualitative research methods to help our students develop and refine their field notetaking and reflective writing.

Qualitative Observations

There are many qualitative methodology texts that feature guide-like information for novice and seasoned researchers interested in conducting field observations. We also find these techniques helpful when working with current teachers as they strive to strengthen their practice as well as when providing guidance to our teacher candidates as they begin to engage in classroom observations. The resources we include here are helpful guides, and we encourage readers to explore research methodology texts as well.

Johnny Saldaña and Matt Omasta (2018) explained that "memory is a sometimes unreliable substitute for credible, tangible evidence" (p. 38), and, thus, detailed field notes are important for documenting what one observes in and beyond the classroom. There are many ways to document what one sees—people might write notes on a laptop, take notes by hand, use drawings or photos, and/or video a session and return to the video as a supplement to the real-time observation (Saldaña & Omasta, 2018). For teachers and teacher candidates, the act of observation is essential to pedagogical and practical growth. Field notes are key to helping teachers and teacher candidates pinpoint salient moments in teaching, as well as pedagogical concerns and questions.

Researcher field notes are a running record of qualitative observations. The documentation of what one sees (e.g., one's observation) is idiosyncratic, as is *how* and *what* one decides to document. If that is the case, then, how might qualitative research methods apply to teacher development and education? In short, qualitative observations involve writing about the human element, and, in what follows, is a suggested approach to a classroom observation that accounts for what the observer sees, hears, feels, and experiences, all which shape interpretation. For teachers and teacher candidates entering the classroom as observers, there are some qualitative research techniques that can be adopted and adapted to support opportunities to "write what you observe as descriptively as possible in the present tense" (Saldaña, 2011, p. 51).

There are several research conventions that are important to include in your observation field notes:

- Be as objective as possible. Write what you observe and keep your personal thoughts separated from what you see. Although your own personal experiences inherently shape how you perceive and record the data, it is important to keep a separate section for the "facts" versus your interpretations, opinions, and/or impressions. Furthermore, Miller and Crabtree (2005) contended that an essential writing strategy includes "*avoiding jargon* and keeping language simple and concrete" (p. 626).
- Acknowledge your biases. As you know from the previous chapters, no texts are neutral. Neither is your observation. Your own experiences somehow will influence your notetaking. It is important to state as plainly as you can how you feel and what biases you bring with you into the space. For instance, Sandra was bullied in her younger years and, therefore, has a heightened sensitivity to student-to-student interaction, microaggressions, and macroaggressions. She remains aware of these sensitivities as she observes, records, and analyzes meaning-making experiences. As you engage in classroom observations, some questions to ask yourself might be: "How do I feel being in this classroom? And why might I feel this way?" These are your feelings, so be honest as you write, but keep these separate from your objective observations. Also, keep track of psychosomatic responses (e.g., headaches, stomach aches, malaise), as well as other physiological responses (e.g., sweat, hunger) that can impact how you *feel*, and, therefore, how you respond to being, in the space on that particular day.
- Keep track of time. Use timestamps (e.g., 12:05pm) when writing field notes. Typically, it is helpful to keep track of time either according to shifts in activity or in five-minute increments, and these times are noted in the space (or margin) adjacent to where you write what you observe. For instance, if you are observing the beginning of Mr. X's class session, your field notes with timestamps might look like this:

> 8:00am—The bell rings, and the students are all sitting at their desks. One student is looking through a bookbag, finds a pen, and places it on top of the desk. The teacher begins by saying, "Good morning," to which the class responds, "Good morning." The teacher notes that there is a prompt on the board and that the students need to free write their responses to it. The prompt on the board is: "There is a saying,

'It is better to have loved and lost than never to have loved at all.'
What do you think that means and how might that apply to the class
reading?"

All but four students begin writing. Two students have their heads
on their desks. The other two are chatting. While the teacher takes
attendance, he reminds students that they need to be writing. The
two students who were talking turn and begin to do so. However, the
students with their heads down slowly sit up.

8:05am—The teacher begins to circulate the room. He points to one
student's paper and gives a thumbs up to the student. The classroom
is quiet, so when the teacher speaks to the students individually, he
whispers, and it is difficult to hear what he is saying.

8:08am—The teacher announces to the class that they have one minute
remaining of their freewriting session, and the students should finish
their thoughts.

8:09am—The teacher asks, "So, what does it mean, 'It is better to have
loved and lost than never to have loved at all?'"

Although five-minute increments are helpful timestamps, instruction is
fluid and flexible, and timestamps might vary. For instance, it is helpful to
use a timestamp to note a shift in instruction (e.g., as shown in the moment
timestamped at 8:08am). Furthermore, if there is an engaging activity and
you are writing feverishly, then the five-minute marker simply might not
work. Rather, if you jot down the time once you are able to, then that will
help to provide a context for the teaching and learning you have observed.
Doing so will provide context to the class session, in general, and each
activity, in particular.

- Consider, what Saldaña and Omasta (2018) called, the "geo-identity" of
  the space, which means that the "site itself [is] an active participant with
  a distinctive character" (p. 39). What are the characteristics or traits of
  the particular space? How will you represent these characteristics in your
  writing and/or drawing of the space? Just as qualitative researchers do,
  teachers and teacher candidates observing a class need to draw a "ground
  plan or bird's-eye view of the field site…hand-drawn to label and assess
  its accommodation of furnishings, spatial relationships, and foot traffic"
  (Saldaña & Omasta, 2018, p. 40). This means sketching the layout of the
  learning space, noting not only where the windows, furniture and lighting
  are, but also where the people are positioned. For the latter, multiple
  sketches might be needed if the layout changes when, for instance, the

Curriculum Matters: Classrooms Are Not Neutral Spaces

As you enter a classroom, take into account that the people in the room have lives outside the four walls and that, for whatever period of time the class runs, these people—the students and the teacher(s)—are expected to focus on the academic content at hand. There can be contrived alignments or even disconnects between in-school and out-of-school practices (cf. Deane, 2018; Erstad & Sefton Green, 2013), and it is important for teachers and teacher candidates to take into account students' experiences and preferences outside school. Furthermore, recognizing that classrooms are not neutral spaces, teachers and teacher candidates need to question:

- What might the arrangement of the classroom furniture indicate about the overall nature of the instruction (e.g., teacher-centered or student-centered instruction)? Are desks in rows facing the teacher's desk or are the desks in groups and the teacher's desk is in a corner? Is the furniture easy to move? How do you know?
- What, if any, efforts are taken to help promote an environment of equity and inclusion? What information is posted on the walls or bulletin boards? What does the teacher say to keep students mindful of others' feelings?
- How do you, as a teacher or teacher candidate and classroom observer, make sure you do not impose your own assumptions when taking notes?
  - Unless the individual self-identifies to you, do not assume a student's or teacher's gender. Rather, just identify the person as a student or teacher.
  - Do not assume a teacher's or student's background based on an accent, skin color, or clothing choice unless the teacher(s) or students specifically talk about their heritage.
  - Remain mindful that you are observing human beings in a classroom for a discrete period of time. Unless the students tell you otherwise, you do not know what happens beyond that timeframe.
  - Likewise, because you are observing human beings, you need to remember that they have feelings and rights, and you have a privilege to learn from the students. Do not exploit them.
- What do you do to honor the students as learners and as teachers? After all, you are learning from them.

teacher asks students to work in dyads and then move their desks from group work to a whole-class circle formation.

In what follows is guidance for teachers and teacher candidates to consider prior to and during their observational roles. As Joseph Maxwell (2013) explained, every plan needs to have some degree of flexibility. Maxwell contended that "the decision you face is not primarily *whether* or *to what extent* you prestructure your study, but *in what ways* you do this, and *why*" (p. 89). For teachers and teacher candidates, this means:

- Thinking about access. Access can address a number of components from actual permission to enter a site to the presence or absence of obstructions to observing student and teacher meaning making. Some questions to consider include:
  - Do you have clearance to observe the space/people?
  - What, if any, legal and unofficial restrictions apply?
  - Will you need written documentation from your professor or administrator to gain access to the space? If so, do not wait until the last minute to ask your professor or administrator for such documentation; having the letter in hand early typically translates into a more prepared and planned approach to classroom observation.
  - How do you anticipate speaking to school officials to ask for permission to engage in observations?
  - Likewise, have you penned a thank you note to the administrator(s) and/or teacher(s) who have agreed to let you visit the classroom? These etiquette components are important because they show appreciation, and, without the collegiality and generosity of administrators, faculty, and staff, teachers and teacher candidates in general would not have the opportunities to learn from experiences in the field.
  - Have you previewed the learning space you will be observing? Are there any physical or auditory barriers to consider? In other words, are there physical obstructions (e.g., support beams, columns), acoustical concerns (e.g., cavernous spaces), or environmental limitations (e.g., heat, cold, sun glares) that might hinder your ability to observe? Consider what happens when you're trying to observe what a teacher or student is doing, but you cannot see because of a sun glare. Or, consider what happens when a teacher is working one-on-one with a student and observing them seems voyeuristic, or it is difficult to hear what they are saying because they are having an individual (instead of small or whole

group) conversation. How, *if at all*, will you note their interaction without interfering with their work and/or creating a sense of discomfort? How, if at all, could you work around/mitigate these concerns?

- Have you spoken with the teacher of record about the classroom culture and the teacher's preferences and expectations for your observation?
- Have you familiarized yourself with the school's protocols and policies for working with or observing students?
- Have you considered your physical positioning in the room (i.e., will you be sitting in a chair in the corner? At a student's desk? At the teacher's desk?) Positioning can impact not only what you see and hear, but also the ways others perceive your role. After all, if you want to get a sense of what it is like to be a student in the classroom, then you will need to sit among the students.

• Thinking about how you have pre-arranged to take notes. This includes approaches to writing the field notes, as well as supplies you plan to use.
- How will you capture the surroundings? Will you craft a rough sketch of the space? Will the school permit you to take pictures or video and, if so, what are the legal limitations?
- Will you take notes by hand? Using a laptop or tablet? Supplementing with video recording? If you choose video recordings, these should not supplant field notes. Rather, as Lichtman (2010) suggested, you should "allow sufficient time immediately after the observation to record your impressions" (p. 168). Furthermore, if you would like to video record the classroom, have you received appropriate permission to do so?
- Does the teacher-of-record have a preference for how you record your notes? Saldaña and Omasta (2018) acknowledged that the clicking of keys when one types might, in fact, cause distraction for the teacher and/or students.
- For the bulk of your notetaking, will you engage in traditional writing, or will you try a using a flowchart-like collection of drawings and descriptions?

Regardless how you capture the space you are observing and the activities within it, you will need to document the Three W's: What? Who? and Where? You will need to identify what you see, including who is present. This means considering where you are in relation to everyone else, where people are gathering, and what is offered in the space. We provide two examples of observational sketches to demonstrate some of the features that you might see in field notes. Figure 2 is a sketch of a university coffee house. Although there is a key to help note what the various markings are, not all field notes need to include a legend or key. However, Figure 3, which provides a wide-angled view of one's movement throughout a maritime museum, provides a legend but does not offer the nuanced details of the observation.

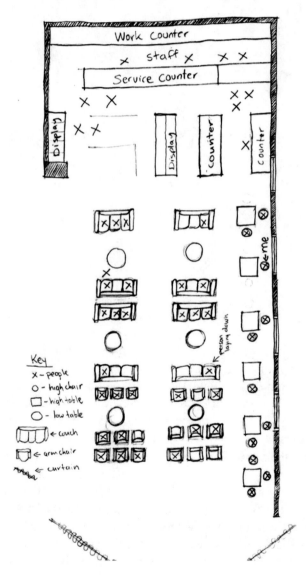

Figure 2. An observation field note sketch of a university coffee house

In Figure 2, the observer identifies the furniture and its layout, marks where individuals are seated or standing, and accounts for fixed items, such as counters or displays. The key in the bottom-left corner helps to remind the observer and any reader what existed in the space and how people organized themselves within the space.

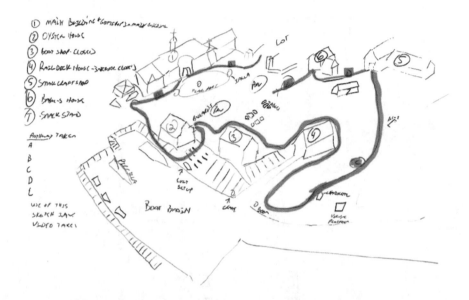

Figure 3. A sketch of one's observation path at a maritime museum

Notice that the sketches of both spaces does not address why, when, or how people are gathering. This is because observation sketches capture the overall setting and do not typically depict the moment-by-moment actions. The latter usually is noted in observation field notes. However, one could attempt action sketches if there is a focus on a particular individual, such as the teacher, and a particular behavior, such as noting where the teacher moves around the room. This is something we see in Figure 4 in which the teacher (noted as "x") moves about a semi-deskless classroom. There are students seated in chairs that are arranged in a horseshoe-style configuration, and there are students seated in groups of four towards the back of the room. Note that not all seats represent where students sit; in the deskless classroom, students have the option to sit where they desire and, as such, there is fluidity and movement. Although this sketch depicts the teacher's movement about the room—starting with x0 (x-zero) and then sequentially with numbers (e.g., x1, x2, x3) showing the advancement and trail of the teacher's path when circulating the room—a similar sketch could be generated to address student movement as well. The latter might be a bit more complicated, but it is possible.

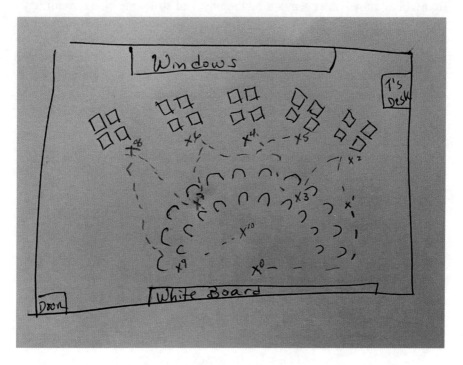

Figure 4. A sample sketch of a teacher's movement around a semi-deskless classroom

What is at the heart of the sketch, however, is the *purpose* of it. When you observe a space—in this case, a classroom—are you focusing on the teacher? The students? A particular student? All of the above? Something else entirely? You cannot be expected to capture *everything* on your own without the use of videorecording device (and, even then, there are limitations). Also, keep in mind that, when you sketch your field notes, you are capturing what already happened. While you are drawing something else is occurring. Do not worry. So long as you have a purpose (or a driving question) in mind, you can maintain your focus and keep assiduous notes, all the while knowing you are remaining on task even if you do not capture every single movement in the room.

At times, sketches can be transferred into digital form. Figure 5 is an example of a library gaming room. The arrows show the directionality of the chairs and the gamers, but it does not show how the youth in the room moved any of the furniture or how they interacted across the tables. What the figure does show, however, is how the physical structures in the room (e.g., the tables, chairs, and television) helped to regulate behavior. For instance, because the television was affixed to the wall, it required the viewer to look and sit a specific way—towards the television—if the viewer were to watch and/or play a videogame. In this case, gamers sat side-by-side or in front/ back of each other. However, at tables where there were board or card games, the activities literally were centered on top of the table, and youth behavior revolved around that focal point.

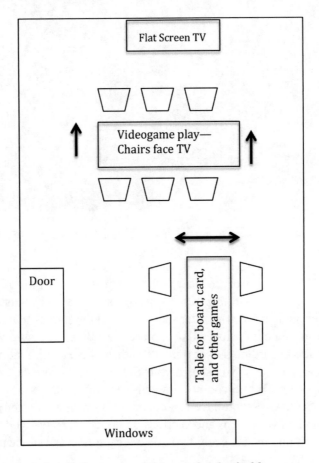

Figure 5. A digital observation field note sketch of a library game space

Across the nondigital and digital sketches, there might be some differences in how structures are represented, as well as the presence or absence of words that identify the structures (e.g., door, counter). However, there is one consistent feature—these sketches do not try to explain why or how people are gathering. Rather they represent only what can be seen (and not what one anticipates or assumes to see). Teachers and teacher candidates might look to this type of observation writing to contextualize their understandings of effective practices and meaning making within formal and informal settings.

Whereas observational sketches provide an overall bird's-eye view of the space, field notes help to fill in the gaps of what one cannot capture in a sketch. This also means:

- Thinking about the five senses. Naturally, you will be documenting what you see, but it also is helpful to note:
  - What you hear. What types of noises are present? Are students talking? Is there a squeaky chair? Are there overhead announcements? These are just some of the noises that exist in and around educational spaces. Documenting teacher and learner responses to these noises will be important as well.
  - What you smell. Sandra and Rick Van Eck engaged in a study of librarians and their gaming programs (2019), and one distinct finding was the smell of teens in a condensed space. Other sources of smells include food, heaters/air conditioners, perfumes/colognes, chemicals (especially in certain science labs), paints and other art supplies, rosin for the bows of stringed instruments or the brass of trumpets, trombones, and tubas in music classes.
  - What you feel. Is the room cold? Hot? Stuffy? If you are sitting at a student's desk, is it firmly on the floor, or is there an imbalance that causes it to rock? Is anything broken? Sandra once sat at a student's desk and tore the side of her pants because there was a sharp piece of metal remaining from a broken desk part. Feeling also can be something sensed, and this type of perceptive work would be noted in the personal thoughts section. Do you sense tension? Exhaustion? Excitement? And, most importantly, why? Here it will be essential to show, not tell, what you mean; thus, you need to be descriptive and use concrete examples to support your documented feelings.
  - What you taste. Every so often, food can be part of a lesson. If that is the case, it will be necessary to record not only what food is used, but also how it tastes to you and how others seem to react to the taste.

Once you have documented what you see, what you hear, what you smell, what you feel, and what you taste (when applicable), it also will be important to note your own positioning. Who you are—from your collective experiences to your physical appearance—can influence how you record and reflect upon your field notetaking experience. These factors also can influence how others perceive you and your presence. For instance, if you are an eighteen-year-old female observing at an all boys' high school, then you might be more acutely aware of your gender difference and proximity in age to the students than if you were to observe a gender diverse first-grade classroom. Likewise, if you do not know any language other than English, and you are observing a Foreign Language class taught solely in that particular language, then you might be hypervigilant of the way the teacher leads the class and the ways the students engage with material at hand given that you are not able to focus on the words being exchanged among the teacher and students. Even when there are situations without such stark contrasts, it will be important to remain acutely aware at all times of your positioning. After all, you are *observing* other people's meaning making, and they are, in one way or another, observing you, too. Although you might not know how all of the students perceive you, you can discuss the ways in which your experiences and physical presence might impact how *you* perceive and record the instruction and the meaning making.

While you are taking field notes, it also is important to explain *without assumptions*. We emphasize this aspect because, almost unknowingly, observers pass judgement about what happens in the classroom. For instance, one teacher candidate was observing an early childhood classroom, and her field notes included the image and explanation noted in Figure 6.

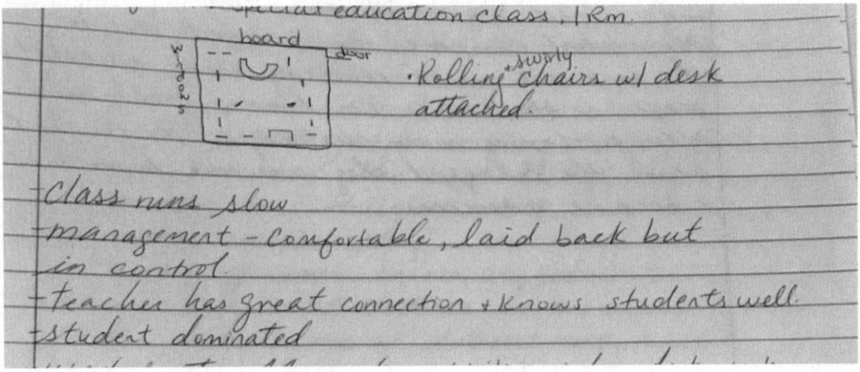

Figure 6. An example of field notes with assumptions rather than explanations

Although the sketch of the classroom shows where the doors, windows, and board are located, it is unclear what the semi-circular object could be: a teacher's desk? A group project table? Although the dashes could indicate desks, that is not certain from the image. Nonetheless, this segment of field notes includes one fact and four opinions. The one fact is that there are "rolling swirly chairs w/desk attached." The other four points are *instantiated* opinions. For instance, what does it mean for a class to "run slow"? Perhaps it seemed slow to the young adult observing an early childhood classroom, but, to the four-year-old, the pace was just right. Or perhaps, the instructional pace really was slow and there was evidence to prove it, such as children's heads resting on the desks or underchallenged children moving ahead to other work. Here, too, is where the inclusion of time stamps would help provide context for the duration of a particular exercise or activity. Likewise, it is unclear what "comfortable" management that is "laid back but in control" might look like. Again, what is considered "comfortable" is subjective. Relatedly, we wonder how the observer knows that the teacher had a "great connection and knows students well." What does that mean? What evidence *proves* that the teacher has such a connection with the students? Does the teacher speak about a particular TV show that many of the children watch? And, if so, does that mean that the teacher knows the students *well*? Also, what does "student dominated" mean, what does it look like, and what evidence supports such an opinion?

Across these questions, there is one constant—the necessity to *show* what happened by using authentic examples (and direct quotes whenever possible) rather than *tell* a story from the observer's point of view. We often suggest to our teacher candidates that their field notes should show, not tell, what they see and be clearly written with supportive evidence so that, if a stranger were to find a copy of the field notes on the street, then that person would be able to understand what the observer *saw* as opposed to what the observer *surmised*. Such is the case in Figure 7, in which the teacher candidate identified what the teacher prepared—"a PowerPoint about the cell of an animal"—as well as what the students were doing: "The student wrote down notes on their iPads using the app 'Notability.'" Although the description of the activity and the students' notetaking could be developed, especially if the teacher candidate were able to see what the notes looked like, the example provides insight into field notetaking that can be accomplished without the comingling of fact and commentary.

The teacher had a PowerPoint made about the cell of an animal. The students wrote down the notes on their iPads using the app "Notability."

Figure 7. An example of field notes without assumptions

Although it is extremely important to state what is seen and not what is assumed, field notes also *should* include areas for interpretation. We call these *comments in the margins* because, literally, you will add your questions, thoughts, assumptions—anything that goes beyond factual reporting—in a left-hand margin or to the left of the red-lined margin if one is using loose leaf paper. Thus, the bottom four notations in Figure 6 actually should be on the left-hand side of the paper, and on the right-hand side should be descriptions about what transpires. This is to avoid accidentally conflating facts and opinion. For example, for the comment about management and/or connection in Figure 6, the observation notes might include: The teacher says, "Now I know you all are looking forward to writing this essay," to which the students laugh. One student says, "You know, Mr. X, we would be happy to relieve you from all that work. We could just tell you what we know about the book." The teacher smiles and tells the students that what they say about the book also is important. However, they need to develop their writing skills and, besides, he "enjoys reading" what the students write.

WHY DO I EVEN NEED TO TAKE FIELD NOTES?

Field notes serve a number of purposes. They enable you to document what you see as you observe teaching and learning in and beyond the classroom. Although you might have an excellent memory, field notes help you to capture what you see in the moment, and, after you have observed a number of classes, the field notes help you to distinguish one observation from another. These noticings then serve as fodder for class discussion, ideas for future instruction, or even reflective thinking about your current and future practice. In what follows, we touch upon each of these components.

Field Notes and Class Discussion

Now that you have a running record of what you saw, the next step will be to debrief about it. This type of first-stage reflection involves talking to your colleagues or classmates about what surprised you and did not surprise you. Here is where the "what happened" (e.g., the facts) will be followed by the "why" (e.g., your thoughts). For instance, you might say that you observed two students with their heads on the desk and you were surprised that the students sat up when the teacher reminded all students to free write. You might explain that this is the first time you have seen a class get back on track with just one notification. Stating aloud such first-step reflections and discussing them with your colleagues or classmates will help to generate (a) questions about pedagogical practices (e.g., how does the teacher do that?) and (b) a mindfulness for future observations (e.g., I am going to watch the teacher's body language more closely next time).

Small group and, when applicable, whole class debriefing discussions also will enable you to hear about what others are observing, how they are interpreting instruction, and the successes and challenges they have experienced. Then, rather than having one field observation solely on paper, there are many observations coming alive through discussion, and there are opportunities to identify similarities and differences in instructional practice and also in field notetaking, offering opportunities for deeper understandings of both. Keeping a professional tone will be important regardless of whether the debriefing is informal or formal.

To be clear, field note debriefs involve sharing your observations. However, it also includes the examination of your colleagues' field notes and the ongoing discussion of their (and your) analyses. It is through such an integrated approach of turn-taking, sharing, and *blending of practices*, that you can refine your own approach to field notetaking. For instance, you might notice how one colleague notes the movement around the classroom using dotted lines, whereas another colleague adopts abbreviations to help improve notetaking efficiencies. These nuanced and personal decisions might also be coupled with comments in the margins that not only include assumptions, but also fold in previous life experiences. Here, you might notice that you had similar thoughts but did not note them, or you might realize that these are new directions to explore. Regardless, what remains important is that such discussion and learning are a process supported by the sharing and, possibly the blending, of experiences and ideas.

Ideas for Future Instruction

In a similar vein, field notes provide a documentation of instruction. You might decide that you really liked how the teacher transitioned from whole class to group work and that you thought the activity in the groups helped each member stay involved and appropriately share the workload. This second-stage reflection involves ideas for applying techniques in your own current or future classroom. For example, imagine that you have read David Barton's (2012) article about how a group of adults documented their lives by taking one photo each day and posting it to the Flicker 365 project. Then, you observe a class in which the students had taken photographs of the stages of their science investigation in an effort to document their procedures and the changes they saw over time. You might notice that images play an important role in students' documenting and reflecting on what happened.

Here, too, you might be inspired to think about how a collection of images—vis-à-vis a storyboard noted in Chapter 3—might help you articulate the practices that you would like to use in your future classroom. A digital story about a particular practice might help to solidify your understandings of the techniques and how you hope to use them when you begin teaching.

FEATURED ASSIGNMENT: REFLECTIVE THINKING ABOUT FUTURE PRACTICE

As you think about your current and future practice, it will be important to document how you have arrived at your current understandings. Here is where you can engage in a deeper reflection that requires you to (a) consider your past experiences, (b) use your own work to document your growth and existing challenges, (c) think about what your knowledge of these factors means in relation to your work as a teacher or teacher candidate, and (d) determine how you can implement such reflective writing in your current and/ or future teaching. This also harkens back to a strategy noted in Chapter 2— gathering multiple sources of evidence. After all, you will be drawing upon your work and citing specific instances of growth, challenge, and opportunity for you as a writer and an educator.

The Featured Assignment, the portfolio, captures the essence of such in-depth reflective writing. What follows is a discussion of the steps involved in completing a portfolio, which includes iterative thinking and writing, as well as the inclusion of evidence to support what is explained. The portfolio challenges you to refer to your own work to show, not tell, the growth you see in your writing and thinking, the challenges you perceive, and the ways you can (and perhaps will) include reflective practices in your current or prospective classroom.

Drawing upon Paulson et al.'s (1991) definition of a portfolio, what we are discussing is:

A purposeful collection of student work that exhibits the student's efforts, progress and achievements in one or more areas. The collection must include student participation in selecting contents, the criteria for selection, the criteria for judging merit and evidence of student self-reflection. (p. 60)

The word, collection, might mislead some to think of the portfolio solely as an archive or repository for completed work. That is not the case; the portfolio showcases the process of growth and learning that you have developed over a specific period of time (e.g., two months, a semester, a year). This can be completed with any subject so long as the longitudinal component is taken into account. With writing, it is especially important to create time and space for your craft to develop. You might need to struggle with an aspect of writing (e.g., explanation, argument, word choice, and/or grammatical issues), begin to work through it, and provide evidence of the struggle (including how you address the struggle) and any subsequent change in your writing. The portfolio is a living, growing collection of your work and *you* carefully select each addition because it specifically demonstrates the learning and progress you have identified in your work. The greatest value of portfolios is that, in building them, you become an active participant in the learning process and its assessment. By reflecting on your own learning (self-assessment), you can identify the strengths and weaknesses in your work and identify goals for improvement.

What is more, the portfolio helps to reinforce the fact that deep and intensive reflection needs to be scaffolded. In the Featured Assignment, there are several steps outlined to help illustrate the multi-levelled nature of reflection. There is the *Gathering and Bird's-Eye Evaluation* level, the first step in which you look at *all* your work and consider what, if anything, stands out immediately. For instance, you might notice similarities in the transitions you use and recognize the need to diversify your approach. Or you might spy changes in how you record educational practice; perhaps your later work includes descriptions of student-to-student classroom interactions, thereby *showing* what you saw, which might be in contrast to your initial work that had superficial recordings.

Given that writing is a process and that you will be reviewing work you have completed over time, there is bound to be some form of visible change. Changes can be small or large, but what is important is that you identify the evolution of your writing. It is possible that there will be distinct differences that stand out to you. Consider the techniques you have tried, what has worked, and what still needs improvement. You might notice larger issues, such as your struggle to synthesize quotes or explain your points to express your original contribution, or your concerns might be granular as you notice your use of a specific word over and over again or the presence of run-on sentences. These are but a few examples, and they can and will be different across each portfolio.

Once you start to notice areas of convergence and divergence in your work, then you are ready to engage in the *Deep Dive and Organization* level, in which, through your examination of your work, you start to articulate main ideas, similarities, and differences, as well as strengths, challenges, and areas for improvement. We recommend creating a separate page for each assignment or activity and then identifying what has changed and what has stayed the same with regard to your writing. However, simply identifying these noticings is not enough. It is essential that, as you look at your work, you find *and highlight* (i.e., using a highlighting marker or the highlight feature in a word processing program) examples and quotes that illustrate and prove the process or progress you have noted in your work. It also will be important for you to then think about how your writing and your noticings relate to your ever-developing pedagogy and practice. More specifically, you will want to consider how your work relates to your goals for improvement and implications for and applications to your teaching or future classroom.

Because the learning portfolio demonstrates your self-assessment of your writing and identification of growth and challenges, at this point—after having engaged in the intensive examination of your own work—you are ready to craft a portfolio analysis essay. This level, the *Arguing for Writing* stage, involves your articulation of what you have witnessed in your own writing in relation to your understanding of the writing process and teaching. *Using your own work as evidence to support your points*, your analysis specifically documents and traces your growth over the course of the noted period of time (e.g., the semester, the year). This includes acknowledging the role of peer review (providing feedback and receiving it from others) and teacher or administrator feedback in your understanding of your strengths and challenges. Keep in mind that your portfolio's contents (including drafts should they help highlight your key points) are your evidence, and you will need to refer to them and give *specific* examples within your essay. The highlighted segments (from the *Deep Dive and Organization* level) not only will help you identify key points, but also will help guide your reader when you refer to specific passages in your writing.

Essentially, as you complete the portfolio, you are applying educational principles of research, theory, and practice because you are exploring and explaining how your work came to be over the course of time. Your inclusion of peer review and teacher/administrator feedback in your consideration of your strengths and weaknesses in your writing also help to exemplify an openness and receptiveness to feedback when you reflect upon the writing and review process, identify goals for improvement, and consider the implications for and applications to your teaching and future classroom.

Although the analysis essay might seem to be the core of the assignment, it is not enough to only reflect upon your learning process and growth. You need to take what you have discovered and apply it, namely to your future writing and your future classroom. This *Implications and Applications* level engages you to think ahead and consider how you can make changes over time and how you can apply similar techniques to your current and/or future teaching. Inherent in this final step is your thinking about the role of writing in education, and we challenge you to resist the portfolio-as-archive sentiment as you consider how writing and reflection are the key to growth in any content area.

Your portfolios can and should vary from another person's portfolio. After all, it is about *your* experiences and *your* interpretations. Nonetheless, it can be helpful to see an example of a teacher or teacher candidate's analysis essay. In what follows are selections from our students' analysis essays. Although the original work has hyperlinked evidence (e.g., the drafts to which the students refer), these have been removed for publication purposes. Notice across the two examples how the students identify what it is that they will focus on based on their *Gathering* and *Deep Dives*, and how they situate their discussion in educational research, theory, and/or practice.

Example of Student Work: Excerpt from Portfolio Analysis Essay A

Teacher feedback and peer review have been two parts of the writing process in this course that have helped me to hone my writing skills. There are two important subtopics of teacher feedback that have helped me develop my writing and show that I have taken into account teacher feedback: language of power and syntax. I will first discuss the language of power and provide evidence to show how my writing has changed by the elimination of language of power in it.

In *Content-Area Writing: Every Teacher's Guide,* Daniels et al. (2007) explained that "An effective teacher models and talks with students about seeking to understand a problem and striving to explain it clearly and convincingly to other people" (p. 121). These strategies that teachers must implement for student success will not be supported if a teacher uses language of power that belittles students or implies that they do not have a choice in the classroom. In question #1 of the first draft of my writing assignment, I use the word *allowing* when referring to student engagement in the video, something I address in my revision. The second example that shows my sensitivity to language of power in writing can be found in blog post #9. I state, "Today's class, especially Dr. [Smith], has me thinking about culturally sensitive writing. This goes hand in hand with language of power and I am thinking about the importance of using language that does not belittle my students in any writing that I am completing (and language of power I am using orally). Sometimes we don't even realize it." I needed to work on my use of language of power in my writing, and I reflected on doing so.

Example of Student Work: Excerpt from Portfolio Analysis Essay B

Throughout the course of this class, we have discussed in depth how the writing process is necessary to achieve good writing. However, by analyzing the writing process more closely, I realized that the writing process is more of a set of guidelines to follow rather than a strict process. After completing the blog posts, discussion threads, and the readings for this course, I have come to two conclusions. The first is that the writing process should be an individual process for each writer. The second conclusion is that the writing process can also be used as a way to promote active learning and collaboration among students.

The writing process can be used as a way to promote student involvement in the lesson and also to promote student collaboration. As I saw displayed in numerous discussion leaders' presentations, writing does not have to be a quiet, solitary activity. It can be a collaborative process that can involve group work or activities involving the whole class. In my discussion post for [David's] discussion leader presentation, I mention how I found his particular activity to be helpful with the prewriting step of the writing process. [David's] activity was that the class was given one word and they were to quickly write down every word that came to their mind by association in the allotted amount of time. This activity is a great way for students to get all of their ideas about the writing assignment out of their heads and on to paper where they can visually see and organize their thoughts into potential topics they would want to write about or include. Not only did this activity help smooth out the prewriting stage of the writing process, it also promoted active learning by engaging the whole class in a short writing activity that they could participate in together. By being an active part of this activity, I got to experience how engaging and helpful it was. As a writer, I personally struggle with getting ideas from my head onto paper in an organized way, and this activity is an excellent way to organize thoughts. I also enjoyed this activity because of its fast-paced nature. Unlike other prewriting techniques, like graphic organizers, this activity was timed, which gave it a sense of urgency. I believe this exhilarated feeling actually helped me produce ideas that were more creative in comparison to organizing my thoughts in a structured chart.

Engendered across these two examples is a distinct noticing of growth, which is accomplished through organized thinking. Notice how the author of Portfolio Analysis Essay A references multiple instances over the course of the semester when she reflected on the language of power. The continuous reflection led to a new and meaningful awareness. Similarly, the author of Portfolio Analysis Essay B draws from in-class activities and discussion posts to develop more refined conclusions regarding the writing process. Keeping key points in mind and referring to your work-as-evidence will help you to craft a strong, cohesive argument about your writing and current and/ or future practice. What is more, organizing your files—perhaps in a cloud-based space, such as Google Drive—will help you develop a collection of your work that can be examined as a whole entity (your work writ large rather than piecemeal) or in light of a particular issue you have identified. What matters is that this organization and articulation of thought helps you to engage in iterative thinking and writing, which considers the past in light of the present and, most importantly, projects a future of transformed, refined, and innovative practice.

PORTFOLIOS AND ASSESSMENT

In this chapter, we present the portfolio as a collection of one's work, and we note that the teacher and teacher candidate's creation *and self-analysis* of the portfolio is an excellent example of process learning through reflection-in-writing and reflection-on-writing, with the writer self-evaluating work and presenting a pattern of growth and/or awareness. Again, we draw your attention to the level of self-reflection and self-evaluation presented in the Analysis Essays as illustrations of this process. Although we represent portfolios through the self-evaluation lens, we would be remiss if we did not at least nod to the fact that portfolios have been used to assess student work in a top-down fashion (e.g., the teacher evaluating the student's work). In this way, a portfolio assessment is a collection of work that supports the student or candidate's progress towards the standards and outcomes that are laid out for that particular discipline. Portfolio assessments are used in PK-12 classrooms as a way to showcase student progress and growth over time. Portfolios can include, but are not limited to, a collection of student work, classroom artifacts, traditional tests, artwork, and writing samples. Whereas these approaches can be helpful in their own right, we argue that teachers and teacher candidates should look for as many opportunities to empower the learner through self-evaluation. Even if rubrics are used (and rubrics can be helpful), we suggest including learners in the creation of the rubric and in the scoring/evaluation of the work.

In recent years, teachers seeking certification also have been involved in the creation of their own portfolio assessments. These portfolio assessments can vary, but most states within the United States adhere to the requirements of the edTPA (Education Teacher Performance Assessment). The edTPA is a subject-specific performance assessment that asks prospective teachers to demonstrate multiple competencies, including the development of authentic lesson plans and teaching materials, the development and analysis of a standards-aligned assessment, the execution of standards-aligned instruction as demonstrated via a teaching video, and the reflection and analysis of teaching performance via written commentaries.

The portfolio is the Featured Assignment in this chapter because we recognize the far-reaching implications of the approach. Whereas you might have seen a strong and useful preview of some of the tasks you will be asked to complete if you participate in the edTPA, we do not intend for any of the Featured Assignments to be preparatory per se. We do *not* believe in teaching to the test. Rather, we trust that the overall goals of the Featured

Assignments—to reflect on and write about teaching practices—will support any work you do in the future that asks you to comment on your own teaching, whether for licensure or not.

CONCLUDING THOUGHTS: FORWARD THINKING

Reflection might hinge on looking backwards and inwards, but it is all about thinking forward and looking toward new and refined understandings that inform your practice. Although this chapter focuses primarily on writing-in-action and writing-on-action as they apply to classroom observation and self-study, these components of reflective writing help to shape the development of one's ethical teaching philosophies and practices. As Bolton (2010) noted, reflective and reflexive practices are ethical in nature; they require the writer to take responsibility for his/her/their words.

Such reflection and responsibility also can be applied to social media and using technology to document, archive, and share ongoing noticings—writing-in-action and writing-on-action—that are part of your educational journey. We contend that, especially with social media, which often lends itself to posting knee-jerk reactions while moving with lightspeed momentum, you remain acutely aware of what you write, why you are writing it, the rationale for posting on social media, and how, if it all, your writing might be misconstrued. Remember, reflecting is not venting. Although you always can engage in reflection-on-writing, with online posts there is little-to-no opportunity to revise without removing the original post, which becomes cached. In other words, there is a permanence to your posts.

Reflection-in-writing and reflection-on-writing also can help you develop and refine your teaching statement, or the overt declaration of your philosophy of teaching and pedagogy. Although this is a formal document, it is a living document, and you can—and should—modify it over the course of your teaching experiences. After all, you are going to think and rethink your practice even if your core beliefs anchor your teaching.

Finally, thinking forward means looking to ways to improve in- and on- practice. This practice can be writing, it can be teaching, and it can be learning. What is important is that you remain open-minded and receptive to feedback, willing to make changes and take (calculated) risks while continuously learning from successes and failures. Current or future students will look to you to understand how writing can figure into their lives; it will be essential for you to embrace the writing and reflective processes and model the humility, excitement, and wonder in the never-ending journey to write and to learn.

Questions for Further Consideration

1. Reflecting can be difficult, especially when there are time constraints. Consider ways that will help to support immediate reflection. Might you capture your reflection as a voice recording on your phone and transcribe it later? Or might you develop shorthand abbreviations to write quickly? Or might you text yourself reflective notes? You might need to experiment with different techniques to find the most appropriate and accurate approach for you.

2. How might engaging in discussions with colleagues or classmates help to further your reflective practices? In other words, before, during, or even after the debriefs, what types of questions might help your colleagues and/ or classmates and you extend your thinking about teaching and learning?

CHAPTER 5

CONCLUSION

> Art : "the quality, production, expression, or realm, according to aesthetic principles, of what is beautiful, appealing, or of more than ordinary significance; a field, genre, or category of art." ("Art," n.d.)

Writing in-and-of itself is an artform. It includes a style that is informed by (but is not limited to) sentence structure, language choice, and expectations (e.g., genre, requirements, freedom or inhibition of expression). In the same way that we might imagine an artistic drawing or painting, writing creates a picture, a complex narrative of ideas and images. We emphasize the word, "art," in our subtitle of this book, *The Art of Writing for Educators*, because we recognize that reflective practice involves much more than simply recording thoughts. Teaching and learning involve human beings of all ages involved in meaning making, and social and cultural expectations abound within and beyond the classroom. In this book, we consider the role of writing in light of teachers' and teacher candidates' personal and professional journeys. And we explore strategies for teaching and learning that are informed by examinations of digital and nondigital meaning making and reflective practices. The art of writing is imbued in practical and theoretical examples threaded throughout this book, and we hope the approaches will inspire life-long personal and professional writing.

The work featured in this book honors the individual as a learner and learning as a process. We contend that this text places the learner at the center of discovery, which is "of more than ordinary significance" ("Art," n.d.). In this case, the learner can be anyone: the teacher candidate, the teacher, the PK-12 student, the family member, the administrator and so on. We all are learners, and meaning making occurs with and *through* writing, be it with pen to paper or fingers to keyboard, alphabetic text or the creation and cohesion of multimodal texts, such as image, sound, and gesture. The (co)creation of meaning is an art that can be developed and refined and is essential to one's role as an educator and a life-long learner.

Your journey as a reader of this text likely brings you to the next question: Where do I go from here? It is our hope that you will build upon the principles

© ELIZABETH CHASE, NANCY P. MORABITO AND
SANDRA SCHAMROTH ABRAMS, 2020 | DOI: 10.1163/9789004437265_005

and practices introduced and developed throughout the book, all the while considering ways to extend understandings of writing as meaning making in and beyond school buildings. In what follows are some examples and insights that should serve as fodder when you consider next steps.

WRITING IN EDUCATION: EXTENDING BEYOND EXPECTATION

In a 2011 issue of *O Magazine*,[1] Maya Angelou explained that there are different ways of being when it comes to writing a poem: "being approached by a poem, or approaching a poem." We contend that writing, overall, is similar. Sometimes we feel the desire to write, and other times we are strapped with the task of writing. Both involve an impetus. Whereas the former evokes a sense of passion-driven writing, the latter implies a prompt-driven effort. Both are inherent aspects of writing, and, in education, we recognize the fact that certain kinds of writing are creative and others are obligatory. Sometimes, there even can be obligatory, creative writing. We contend that the ideas and information in this book can help you achieve the obligatory and embrace the creative.

Take, for instance, one of our students who focused on tattoos and body art as examples of writing in general and embodied writing in particular. On her left calf, the student had a tattoo of a letter her father had written to her. The image even preserved the style specific to her father's cursive handwriting. This is similar to the tattoo-as-writing noted in the digital story (see the Featured Assignment in Chapter 3) in which students explained that "Tattoos are used to express identity by honoring people that shaped that person's life and to keep those people close. The text chosen for tattoos represents something important to the person" (Morabito & Abrams, 2015, p. 70). What is more, these students also chose to foreground a tattoo as a way to remember one who had passed and memorialize a life event. In this case, the tattoo was a replica of a prayer card from the student's grandfather's funeral service.

In this anecdote, one can see how people make meaning through an expansive understanding of writing that is both creative and provocative. We recognize that writing can be formulaic. The five-paragraph essay—the quintessential example of obligatory writing—involves an opening and closing paragraph sandwiching three supportive paragraphs, each with its own example and quotes to prove the thesis. In fact, often a sandwich graphic organizer is used to help students develop their writing and conceptualize how the five paragraphs cohere. Knowing how to write a five-paragraph essay is important because it establishes a shared framework for communicating ideas. Although the five-paragraph essay is a convention, it is also a constraint in many cases. Nonetheless, it is a convention that requires great facility in order to be iterated upon. How can students defy convention if they do not know what it is?

The Featured Assignments presented across the chapters offer opportunities for authentic and flexible writing. Calling upon the examples throughout this book, and more recently of the tattoos, we ask that you consider ways that your students and you can see writing as something that extends beyond words. If the focus is not on words on a page, but, rather, meaning making that is nuanced, complex, and difficult, then there are opportunities to create and (re)invent forms of writing and communication. For instance, e.e. cummings, who is well known for writing in all lowercase (among other stylistic choices), shows us that writing can deviate from the norm in both subtle and distinguishable ways. Writing can be enjoyable, and it can involve forward thinking. It can be cheeky, and it can be fun.

EXTENDING BEYOND EXPECTATION: ADVOCACY AND WRITING

This book goes beyond reference guides and lesson planning outlines, and instead, gets at the heart (and art) of understanding writing in education. In the preceding chapters, we provide an exploration and explanation of many different forms of writing and why they are important. We recognize that some books about writing and teaching might focus more closely on templates (such as lesson plan formats), but we intentionally move beyond those offerings because what we present to you goes deeper than templates and mechanics. Writing is both personal and professional, and experiences and intentions inform one's craft. We contend that teachers and teacher candidates can (and should) leverage writing to grow and develop their pedagogical practice.

What we want to emphasize herein is that it is important not to get caught in the mire of the how-to of writing (i.e., how to write grammatically correct sentences, how to write a lab report). Although the how-to *is* important, this book goes beyond what you would learn in a first-year writing class (e.g., how to write in a more academic manner for higher education classes), beyond what you would learn in a course on teaching writing in the PK-12 classroom (e.g., methods and strategies for teaching writing to your students), and beyond what you would learn as you work towards improving your writing instruction as an educator (e.g., a professional development course on writing instruction). Although there is value in developing content-specific writing, such as writing a science lab report or a response to a document-based question (DBQ) for history class, it is very different from profession-specific writing in education, which includes, but is not limited to, letters to administrators and reflective pieces in professional portfolios. Such professional writing not only helps to refine and strengthen communication among stakeholders (e.g., faculty, administrators, students, families), but also helps to advocate for enriched educational experiences for PK-12 students and partnerships with families/guardians.

These skills can be applied to other professional writing. For instance, the skills and practices noted in Chapter 2 can be put to use in grant writing or national board certification applications. Being able to convey clearly what you are doing and why you are doing it has material consequences, namely that you can advocate (or refine your advocacy) for students and present clearer lines of communication with key stakeholders. What we suggest is the possibility that a more expansive understanding of writing-as-meaning-making holds the possibility for transformative change. This change comes about as a result of embracing writing as a force that holds power of expression, of reflection, and of multi-dimensional meaning. In this way, writing lifts the traditional five-paragraph essay off of the page and enables teachers and teacher candidates to create writing spaces and classroom environments that acknowledge the voices of all learners rather than just those who excel in traditional forms of writing. In this way, we view the art of writing in education as a democratic approach to meaning making, as a way to address the expressions of all learners, and as a tool for creating permanent and inclusive writing structures in your classroom.

EXTENDING BEYOND EXPECTATION: WRITING AND THE CLASSROOM

The ideas presented in this book stem from an undergraduate class we three developed and co-taught, and from our experiences as educators and writers. Throughout the chapters, we highlight the value of writing in a variety of forms. The Featured Assignments described in Chapters 2, 3, and 4 ask you to engage in very different types of writing and communication: responding to targeted prompts to explore teaching practices, creating a digital story to explore writing, and reflecting upon and writing about your own understandings of writing and teaching through the creation of a portfolio, respectively. In this way we strive to lead by example, encouraging our students and you, our reader, to stretch your thinking about what writing in education is, what it can be, and how embracing a more expansive view of writing can serve your students and you. What is more, we underscore the *art of writing for educators* because we recognize that this involves the integration of pedagogical craft, context awareness, and cross-literate practices.

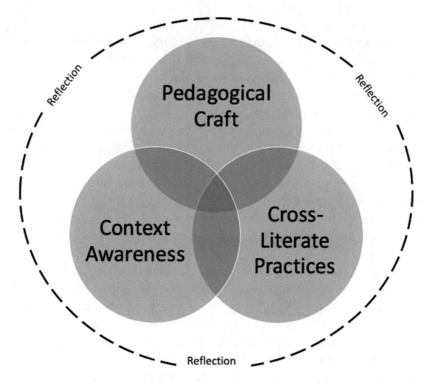

Figure 8. The elements of the art of writing for educators

To help you envision ways to extend writing beyond expectation, we offer the image in Figure 8 to demonstrate how the art of writing for educators hinges on the delicate balance of three domains. First, pedagogical craft pertains to educational practices that are supported by sound theory and experience (such as modelling writing practices for students). Second, context awareness acknowledges how meaning is socially and culturally situated. Thus, context awareness accounts for who is writing and reading the work, when it is being written and read, and how the work might be interpreted. Third, the concept of cross-literate practices acknowledges the various experiences and content that writers draw upon to make meaning. Envisioning and applying such content understandings in concert with personal meaning yields writing that is authentic and purposeful.

Whereas each of these three domains is a vital component of this framework in its own right, it is the point of convergence among them, as well as the manner in which reflection envelopes all three elements both individually and collectively, that truly speaks to the *art* of writing for educators. It is laudable to account for one's pedagogical craft and instructional decision making, remaining aware of the situatedness of any form of text, and intentionally engaging students in cross-literate practices to support meaning making and understanding; however, what is most desirable is teaching and learning at the nexus in Figure 8, as well as continuously reflecting upon this nexus in order to improve one's practice.

Take, for instance, the word, tangent. In geometry, it refers to "A line that touches a circle or ellipse at just one point," ("Tangent," n.d.), and, in trigonometry, "In a right triangle, the tangent of an angle is the opposite side over the adjacent side" ("Tangent," n.d.). These two definitions are different from a tangent, or an unrelated thread or idea, which often is part of informal conversation and brainstorming. As much as meaning can be context and content area specific, there are opportunities to bridge and enrich meaning making, extend beyond silos, and interconnect experiences, understandings, and practices. We suggest that, for teachers and teacher candidates, the craft in writing involves forward thinking that remains focused on the meaning making as opposed to navigating the labyrinth of obligatory structures. Reflective practice is essential for developing, re-envisioning, and refining almost any practice in general and the art of writing in particular. With this framework for writing in education, we contend that teachers and teacher candidates can create possibilities for themselves as teachers and learners and, thus, create possibilities for current and future students.

As we noted in the Introduction, this book—and the skills, resources, and assignments within—required a certain amount of openness to change. That is, we approached writing from a perspective that went beyond a five-paragraph essay and instead invited a more expansive, reflective view of what it means to embrace meaning making in the classroom. The question remains: how do you use what you have learned within this book to continue to grow and build both your understandings and capacities for reflective writing and meaning making? We have held space for you, the reader, to see writing in education differently, and now the possibilities for what to do with that information are up to you. It is our hope that Figure 8 will support you in your forward-thinking pedagogical journeys.

EXTENDING BEYOND EXPECTATION: WHERE TO GO FROM HERE

To conclude, we offer some reflections on what we, as teacher educators, have done with our new understandings of reflective writing and meaning making as a result of having taught this course over many semesters, as well as having put this book together. Here are some of our positions and suggestions:

- We see writing as an opportunity for expansive meaning making.
- We believe that strong writing positions teachers and teacher candidates as advocates for themselves and their students.
- We support writing that evolves not only with the learner, but also with (and despite) the context.
- We value writing instruction that values the writer's experiences and the art in the practice.
- We understand that the art of writing for educators involves the balance of pedagogy, content area knowledge, and cross-literate practices, and that, because writing is human, this balance can and will vary across classrooms.
- Although we all work within the demands of various institutional structures, we push back against the business (or busy-ness) of filling in blanks, photocopying worksheets, and following scripted curricula without recursion, revision, or reinvention. Instead, we are in the business of empowering teachers and teacher candidates (and ultimately, their students) through writing by exploring how meaning can manifest itself in various modalities, styles, and iterations.

We ask you, the reader, to be open to envisioning:

- Writing and social change
- Writing *for* social change
- Writing as a pervasive activity—from the moment you wake up until the moment you go to sleep (and sometimes even occurring in your sleep)
- More ways of meaning making
- Seeing writing as something beyond paper and pencil and something beyond the five-paragraph essay
- Writing as something beyond the "unit"

Thus, we ask you to (re)invent writing in your lives as teachers and as learners and to explore how you will embrace the art of writing in your classroom and in your life. To help you think about your journey of discovery in this book, we invite you to reflect on and consider the following questions:

- What are you? Are you a writing teacher, a teacher who teaches writing, a writer who teaches, or some other combination?
- What part(s) of this book resonate with you? Why?
- What do you envision doing with this new knowledge?
- Where do you envision getting stuck?
- What other pedagogical inquiry might you be willing to explore?
- What do you see differently now?

These questions are invitations to think about your identity as a teacher and as a writer, and, in particular, about how these two identities merge in your professional life as an educator.

CONCLUDING THOUGHTS

Writing is an artform and, thus, needs to be treated as such in and beyond the classroom. Embracing the art of writing in education translates into practices that honor individual life experiences and cross-literate connections, while drawing upon pedagogical craft and content awareness. This is both complex and exciting because possibilities abound in the nuances of individual and collective expression and meaning making. We strongly encourage teachers and teacher educators to pursue and embrace ongoing reflective practices *and* to share the approaches that are or are not working, identify the supports and barriers, and consider avenues to sustain and promote effective practices and refine troubling ones. Furthermore, we suggest that a troubling or arduous approach might simply need retooling as opposed to complete abandonment. Teachers and teacher educators can look to the resources and techniques addressed in this book—from peer review to self-reflection—to create and develop authentic, meaningful, and artful writing experiences.

We hope that, by conceptualizing writing as an artform, you will approach writing in education as a series of opportunities for rich and engaging meaning making. This requires an openness to change and a willingness to embrace writing as a recursive practice. This kind of openness can breathe new life into tired instructional techniques that rest on a status quo. And, yet, this kind of openness also can be unfamiliar and uncomfortable. We argue that discomfort engenders change and growth, and, therefore, we suggest that this change is worth a try. We began this book with an image of writing that is comically pervasive: children hunched at desks, pencils tethered to worksheets or notebooks. We end this book with an invitation to embrace a new vision, one that is rooted in the more expansive exploration of writing that you have journeyed through in this text. From rationalizing pedagogy to cross-literate practices to reflective writing, we invite you to explore writing in education as a way to create understandings and effect change. And, most of all, we ask that you be part of the evolution of writing by envisioning meaning making as dynamic, gratifying, and artful.

NOTE

[1] Read more: http://www.oprah.com/spirit/how-to-write-a-poem-maya-angelous-advice/all#ixzz65errLauk

ABOUT THE AUTHORS

Elizabeth (Liz) Chase (Ed.D.): Throughout the many twists and turns of my academic life, there remains one constant: I love being a student. I find classrooms to be generative spaces, places where I can experiment, dream, think and develop. Although it was not probable that I would spend my life as a student, it was entirely possible that I would craft a professional life as an educator so that I could remain in classrooms. After graduating from college, I earned my master's degree in Education and I taught middle school students for ten years. After eight of those teaching years, I began my doctoral studies at Teachers College, Columbia University and also transitioned into an administrative role wherein I orchestrated and supported teacher development at my middle school. Upon completing my doctoral work, I joined the School of Education at St. John's University, where I teach a range of courses, including the one that serves as the inspiration and motivation for this book, *The Art of Writing for Educators*. Most importantly, as Assistant Professor in the Department of Curriculum and Instruction at St. John's University, I have the opportunity to develop new ideas alongside inspiring teacher candidates both in the classroom and in the field.

Nancy P. Morabito (Ph.D.): As an undergraduate majoring in biology, I found little opportunity to explore my interests in teaching. Thus, I was immersed in the field of education in earnest when I began my master's degree studies in secondary science teaching. After teaching at the high school level (specifically, courses in biology, human anatomy and physiology, and AP biology), I pursued my Ph.D. in Learning, Teaching, and Diversity with a specialization in science education at Vanderbilt University. Soon after joining the faculty at St. John's University, I became involved with the co-development and co-teaching of *The Art of Writing for Educators*, as this course was originally designed to be co-taught by a faculty member with expertise in ELA/writing and a faculty member with expertise in a different content area. As Associate Clinical Professor in the Department of Curriculum and Instruction, my research interests primarily focus on science teacher education and development, as well as writing in the science classroom.

Sandra Schamroth Abrams (Ph.D.): When I was in fifth grade, we completed an activity in which we identified (or likely guessed) our future profession. I indicated that I would be an educator, a path that seemed predetermined for me because, despite my explorations of other fields, I continuously found myself in schools or academic settings working with students, teachers, administrators, and families. I even tutored throughout my high school, undergraduate, and graduate years. When completing my master's in Literature, I enrolled in a year-long Teaching of Writing program and co-taught undergraduate writing classes. Eventually, when I realized that teaching was, in fact, my established direction, I completed my master's in Education and became a high school English and writing educator. After a number of years in the field, I returned to the university classroom, first for my Ph.D. from Rutgers, The State University of New Jersey (where I also co-directed the National Writing Project) and then as a full-time faculty member at St. John's University. Currently, as Professor of Adolescent Education in the Department of Curriculum and Instruction, my research includes working with and learning from high school and middle school faculty and students, and refining my understandings of literacies, pedagogies, and practices.

REFERENCES

Abrams, S. S. (2015). *Integrating virtual and traditional learning in 6–12 classrooms: A layered literacies approach to multimodal meaning making.* Routledge.

Abrams, S. S. (2017). Emotionally crafted experiences: Layering literacies in *Minecraft. The Reading Teacher, 70*(4), 501–506.

Abrams, S. S., & Gerber, H. R. (2014). Cross-literate connections: Contemporary frames for meaning making in ELA classrooms. *English Journal, 103*(4), 18–24.

Abrams, S. S., & Van Eck, R. (2019, December). *Illuminating the present and future of videogame programming and literacy practices in US libraries.* Paper presented at the Literacy Research Association meeting, Tampa, FL.

Anderson, J. D. (1988). *Education of Blacks in the South, 1860–1955.* University of North Carolina Press.

Arroyo, C. (n.d.). *Angry birds project.* Retrieved from https://ab4christopherarroyo.weebly.com/forces--newtons-laws.html

Art. (n.d.). In dictionary.com. Retrieved from https://www.dictionary.com/browse/art?s=t

Barnes, M. E., & Smagorinsky, P. (2016). What English/language arts teacher candidates learn during coursework and practica: A study of three teacher education programs. *Journal of Teacher Education, 67*(4), 338–355. https://doi.org/10.1177/0022487116653661

Barton, D. (2006). Significance of a social practice view of language, literacy and numeracy. In L. Tett, M. Hamilton, & Y. Hillier (Eds.), *Adult literacy, numeracy, and language: Policy, practice, and research* (pp. 21–30). Open University Press McGraw Hill Education.

Barton, D. (2012). Participation, deliberate learning and discourses of learning online. *Language and Education: An International Journal, 26*, 139–150.

Boaler, J. (2015). *Mathematical mindsets: Unleashing students' potential through creative math, inspiring messages and innovative teaching.* John Wiley & Sons.

Bolton, G. (2010). *Reflective practice: Writing & professional development* (3rd ed.). Sage Publications Inc.

Brookfield, S. D. (2015). *The skillful teacher: On technique, trust, and responsiveness in the classroom.* John Wiley & Sons.

Bruce, D. L. (2008). Visualizing literacy: Building bridges with media. *Reading and Writing Quarterly, 24*(3), 264–282.

Burnett, C., Merchant, G., Pahl, K., & Rowsell, J. (2014). The (im)materiality of literacy: The significance of subjectivity to new literacies research. *Discourse: Studies in the Cultural Politics of Education, 35*(1), 90–103.

Chigona, A. (2013). Using multimedia technology to build a community of practice: Pre-service teachers and digital storytelling in South Africa. *International Journal of Education and Development using Information and Communication Technology, 9*(3), 17–27.

Cockett, A., & Kilgour, P. W. (2015). Mathematical manipulatives: Creating an environment for understanding, efficiency, engagement, and enjoyment. *Teach Collection of Christian Education, 1*(1), 5.

Colonnese, M. W., Amspaugh, C. M., LeMay, S., Evans, K., & Field, K. (2018). Writing in the disciplines: How math fits into the equation. *The Reading Teacher, 72*(3), 379–387.

REFERENCES

Cope, B., Kalantzis, M., & Abrams, S. S. (2017). Multiliteracies: Meaning-making and learning in the era of digital text. In F. Serafini & E. Gee (Eds.), *Remixing multiliteracies: Theory and practice from New London to new times* (pp. 35–49). Teachers College Press.

Daniels, H., Zemelman, S., & Steineke, N. (2007). *Content-area writing: Every teacher's guide*. Heinemann.

Deane, P. (2018). The challenges of writing in school: Conceptualizing writing development within a sociocognitive framework. *Educational Psychologist, 53*(4), 280–300.

Delpit, L. (2006). *Other people's children: Cultural conflict in the classroom*. The New Press.

Doering, A., Beach, R., & O'Brien, D. (2007). Infusing multimodal tools and digital literacies into an English education program. *English Education, 40*(1), 41–60.

Elbow, P. (1998). *Writing with power: Techniques for mastering the writing process*. Oxford University Press.

EngageNY.org of the New York State Department of Education. (2016). *NYS K-8 social studies framework* [PDF file]. Retrieved from https://www.engageny.org/resource/new-york-state-k-12-social-studies-framework

Erstad, O., & Sefton-Green, J. (2013). Digital disconnect? The 'digital learner' and the school. In O. Erstad & J. Sefton-Green (Eds.), *Identity, community, and learning lives in the digital age* (pp. 87–103). Cambridge University Press.

Falk, B., & Blumenreich, M. (2012). *Teaching matters: Stories from inside city schools*. The New Press.

Fletcher, R., & Portalupi, J. (2001). *Writing workshop: The essential guide*. Heinemann.

Flower, L., & Hayes, J. R. (1981). A cognitive process theory of writing. *College Composition and Communication, 32*(4), 365–387.

Freire, P. (1972). *Pedagogy of the oppressed* (M. B. Ramos, Trans.). Herder.

Graham, S., & Perin, D. (2007). *Writing next: Effective strategies to improve writing of adolescents in middle and high schools – A report to Carnegie Corporation of New York*. Alliance for Excellent Education.

Gray, K., & Koncz, A. *The key attributes employers seek on students' resumes*. National Association of Colleges and Employers. Retrieved from https://www.naceweb.org/about-us/press/2017/the-key-attributes-employers-seek-on-students-resumes/

Gillespie, T. (1985). Becoming your own expert: Teachers as writers. *The National Writing Project Network Newsletter, 8*(1), 1–2.

hooks, b. (2014). *Teaching to transgress: Education as the practice of freedom*. Routledge.

Heo, M. (2009). Digital storytelling: An empirical study of the impact of digital storytelling on pre-service teachers' self-efficacy and dispositions toward educational technology. *Journal of Educational Multimedia and Hypermedia, 18*(4) 305–428.

Hobbs, R., & Jensen, A. (2009). The past, present, and future of media literacy education. *Journal of Media Literacy Education, 1*, 1–11.

Hobbs, R., & Moore, D. C. (2013). *Discovering media literacy: Teaching digital media and popular culture in elementary school*. Corwin.

Hughes, L. (1936, July). Let America be American again. *Esquire Magazine*.

Koltay, T. (2011). The media and the literacies: Media literacy, information literacy, and digital literacy. *Media, Culture & Society, 33*, 211–221.

Kress, G. (2010). *Multimodality: A social semiotic approach to contemporary communication*. Routledge.

Lewin, T. (2003, April). Writing in schools is found both dismal and neglected. *The New York Times*. Retrieved from https://www.nytimes.com/2003/04/26/us/writing-in-schools-is-found-both-dismal-and-neglected.html

Lichtman, M. (2010). *Qualitative research in education: A user's guide*. Sage Publications Inc.

Livingstone, S., & van der Graaf, S. (2010). Media literacy. In W. Donsbach (Ed.), *The international encyclopedia of communication*. doi:10.1002/9781405186407.wbiecm039

Maxwell, J. (2013). *Qualitative research design: An interactive approach* (3rd ed.). Sage Publications Inc.

Miller, S. M. (2007). English teacher learning for new times: Digital video composing as multimodal literacy practice. *English Education, 40*(1), 61–83.

Miller, W., & Crabtree, B. (2005). Clinical research. In N. Denzin & Y. Lincoln (Eds.), *Handbook of qualitative research* (3rd ed., pp. 605–639). Sage Publications Inc.

Moll, L. C., Amanti, C., Neff, D., & Gonzalez, N. (1992). Funds of knowledge for teaching: Using a qualitative approach to connect homes and classrooms. *Theory into Practice, 31*(2), 132–141.

Morabito, N. P., & Abrams, S. S. (2015). Digital storytelling: A tool to develop pre-service teachers' cross-literate reflections. In E. Ortlieb, L. Shanahan, & M. McVee (Eds.), *Video as a tool for reflection in literacy education and research* (pp. 59–77). Emerald Group.

Morgan, D. N. (2010). Preservice teachers as writers. *Literacy Research and Instruction, 49*(4), 352–365.

Morgan, D. N., & Pytash, K. E. (2014). Preparing preservice teachers to become teachers of writing: A 20-year review of the research literature. *English Education, 47*(1), 6–37.

Murdoch, H. A. (2009). A legacy of trauma: Caribbean slavery, race, class, and contemporary identity in "Abeng." *Research in African Literatures, 40*(4), 65–88.

National Association for Media Literacy Education. (n.d.). *Media literacy defined*. Retrieved from https://namle.net/publications/media-literacy-definitions/

National Governors Association Center for Best Practices and Council of Chief State School Officers. (2010). *Common core state standards*. http://www.corestandards.org

NGSS Lead States. (2013). *Next generation science standards: For states, by states*. The National Academies Press.

New London Group. (1996). A pedagogy of multiliteracies: Designing social futures. *Harvard Educational Review, 66*(1), 60–92.

Ohler, J. (2013). *Digital storytelling in the classroom: New media pathways to literacy, learning and creativity* (2nd ed.). Corwin Press.

Orwell, G. (2005). *Why I write*. Penguin.

Paulson, F. L., Paulson, P. R., & Meyer, C. A. (1991). What makes a portfolio a portfolio? *Educational Leadership, 58*(5), 60–63.

Potter, W. J. (2019). *Media literacy* (9th ed.). Sage Publications Inc.

Rosenblatt, L. M. (1994). The transactional theory of reading and writing. In R. R. Ruddell, M. R. Rudell, & H. Singer (Eds.), *Theoretical models and processes of reading* (4th ed., pp. 1057–1092). International Reading Association.

Saldaña, J. (2011). *Fundamentals of qualitative research: Understanding qualitative research*. Oxford University Press.

Saldaña, J. (2016). *The coding manual for qualitative researchers* (3rd ed.). Sage Publications Inc.

REFERENCES

Saldaña, J., & Omasta, M. (2018). *Qualitative research: Analyzing life.* Sage Publications Inc.
Schön, D. A. (1983). *The reflective practitioner: How professionals think in action.* Routledge.
State Education Agency Directors of Arts Education. (2014). *National core arts standards: Visual arts at a glance* [PDF file]. Retrieved from http://www.nationalartsstandards.org/sites/default/files/Visual%20Arts%20at%20a%20Glance%20rev.pdf
Street, B. V. (1999). Literacy and social change: The significance of social context in the development of literacy programmes. In D. A. Wagner (Ed.), *Future of literacy in a changing world* (pp. 55–72). Hampton Press.
Tangent. (n.d.). In *Math open resource.* Retrieved from https://www.mathopenref.com/tangent.html
Totten, S. (2005). Writing to learn for preservice teachers. *The National Writing Project Quarterly, 27*(2), 17–19.
Vent. (n.d.). In *Merriam-Webster.* Retrieved from https://www.merriam-webster.com/dictionary/vent
Wiggins, G., & McTighe, J. (2006). *Understanding by design* (expanded 2nd ed.). Pearson.

INDEX